CLIMBING THE HILL

CLIMBING
THE HILL

HOW TO BUILD A CAREER
IN POLITICS AND MAKE
A DIFFERENCE

JAIME HARRISON
and AMOS SNEAD

TEN SPEED PRESS
California | New York

CONTENTS

PREFACE

A Republican and a Democrat, a love of politics, and some fortuitous blazers. This isn't the setup to a bad joke. This is the story of how each of us went from small-town Southern boys with dreams of careers in politics to working for some of the biggest names in Congress.

So how did we get to Washington?

Let's begin with Jaime, who grew up the son of a single mother in Orangeburg, South Carolina. A small, rural town, Orangeburg (population 13,000) was about as far away from the Washington sphere—socially, if not geographically—as one could get. In his neighborhood, few people talked about politics; fewer had been to Washington.

Jaime's mother was just a teen when she had him and had to drop out of school to take care of him. She eventually moved to Atlanta to find a job that would help support her and her young son. Jaime remained in South Carolina with his grandparents. His grandparents did not have much formal education; his grandmother's ended after eighth grade, and his grandfather's ended after fourth grade. Nonetheless his grandfather was a voracious consumer of news, who watched the morning and evening news every day. You must remember that this was about twenty years before the advent of the internet, when everyone, from Orangeburg to Washington to Los Angeles, got their news from three sources: the newspaper, radio, and television. So Jaime began to watch the news with his grandfather, taking in the happenings of a world far beyond his tiny town.

Jaime soon became interested in the presidency. His first real political memory is watching the 1988 Democratic National Convention in Atlanta, particularly the Reverend Jesse Jackson's speech before the delegates. Though he had more than 1,200 delegates, Jackson lost the nomination to Massachusetts Governor Michael Dukakis, but his second-place finish in the primaries ensured a prime speaking role for the most prominent African American politician of the day.

Jackson spoke on the second day of the convention, July 19, just before 11 p.m., which, on a school night no less, was well past Jaime's bedtime. But Jaime would always remember Jackson's speech—much more than he would remember Dukakis's acceptance speech two nights later. Rereading Jackson's speech now, it's no wonder the memory stuck with him.

> *America is not a blanket woven from one thread, one color, one cloth. When I was a child growing up in Greenville, South Carolina, my grandmama could not afford a blanket, she didn't complain and we did not freeze....*
>
> *Young America, hold your head high now. We can win. We must not lose to the drugs, and violence, premature pregnancy, suicide, cynicism, pessimism and despair. We can win. Wherever you are tonight, now I challenge you to hope and to dream. Don't submerge your dreams.*

This was inspiring stuff to a poor black kid, who also happened to be from South Carolina. From that moment on, Jaime remembers, he caught the politics bug. Four years later, in 1992, he joined the Young Democrats of South Carolina and volunteered to help the Clinton-Gore campaign at the county fair. A year or so after that, Jaime applied for and was accepted into the Hearst Foundations' United States Senate Youth Program. As one of two student "delegates" representing South Carolina, Jaime visited Washington, DC, for the first time. If Jackson's speech was Jaime's first political moment, his visit to Washington was the moment that changed his life.

Touring the nation's capital with his fellow "delegates," Jaime visited the White House, where he met White House Chief of Staff Thomas "Mack" McLarty, and at the Justice Department he had the chance to ask US Attorney General Janet Reno about how she got into politics. He received a briefing at the Pentagon by General John Shalikashvili, chair of the Joint Chiefs of Staff, and he sat in the Speaker's chair on the floor of the House of Representatives. None of these encounters are on the usual tours, by the way.

But when Jaime was supposed to meet with the senators from South Carolina, he had a problem. He hadn't brought a blazer. He ended up borrowing one from a member of the special military escort responsible for taking the kids around town—and that guy had to go home to get it. It was Jaime's first, but certainly wouldn't be his last, vintage Washington moment (that is, when, amid crisis, everything works out somehow).

Beyond the meetings, briefings, and close scrapes, Jaime experienced a life he had no idea existed, certainly not in his tiny town of Orangeburg. It was more than the glamour and gilt, although there was plenty of that. (With his fellow high school "delegates," Jaime stayed at the Mayflower Hotel, as ritzy a place as one will find in Washington. The TV in his bathroom so impressed Jaime that he called his mother to tell her about it.) Rather, for the first time in his life Jaime was meeting with and talking to people who shared his interests. And they were his own age, unlike his grandfather. Very few of his peers in his hometown talked much about politics, and certainly no one expressed a passion for politics in the way he encountered on his Washington trip. He wasn't alone after all. Here he found people from all over the country (every state in fact) who were just like him. They might have come from different backgrounds, ethnicities, or social circumstances, but they were "his" people, in that they all shared a passion for Washington and Capitol Hill.

The trip changed Jaime's life. He knew now what he wanted to do with his life and where he wanted to do it.

Amos's story is similar to Jaime's in that it was a trip to Washington that changed his life. But before we get ahead of ourselves, first a little bit of Amos's background. Like Jaime, Amos is a child of the South, having grown up in the town of Centre (population 3,500) in northeast Alabama. His upbringing was humble, although far from poor. His world was constricted, although that never occurred to Amos growing up. Alabama was home for him and, in many ways, still is.

When Amos was a boy, he assisted his grandfather at the family country store, Famous Amos Fireworks. The store was an especially popular one just across the border, in Georgia. Meeting and selling to people from all walks of life, Amos learned a powerful tool: the gift of gab. He learned how to talk to anyone about anything (so long as they bought something).

Amos's interest in politics was sparked at a young age. When he was in high school, he was given an opportunity through a family friend to visit Washington, DC, and have a short stint volunteering in a Senate office. From his volunteer work, Amos was able to secure an internship in the office of Senator Richard Shelby from Alabama during the summer before his senior year in high school.

We can set the stage of Amos's first visit to Washington thus: First, he had never been on a plane before. Second, he didn't have a blazer for his first intern meeting with Shelby's staff. Third, he was still in high school. Even at the high threshold allowed to interns for rookie mistakes, Amos was woefully unprepared. For instance, when the other interns cited where they were going (or went) to school, Amos blurted out "Cherokee High School!" He didn't realize they were talking about colleges and not high schools.

But Amos quickly discovered that he had one thing some of his fellow interns didn't: the ability, and desire, to talk to people. That old store gab, Amos realized, worked as well in Washington as it did in the family shop. Perhaps it's because Washington, as John F. Kennedy famously observed, is a city of "Southern efficiency and Northern charm." His peers, his superiors, and those he didn't know at all liked the wide-eyed Southern kid who didn't know that he shouldn't be charming everyone he met.

Much like Jaime, however, what most impressed Amos as a teenager working on Capitol Hill was the explosion of life that he never knew existed. It was a world unlike anything he had imagined. During his senior year in high school, Amos read *The Great Gatsby*, and in the descriptions of Gatsby's fabulous parties he finally found the words to match his own, albeit brief, Capitol Hill experience.

> *The lights grow brighter as the earth lurches away from the sun, and now the orchestra is playing yellow cocktail music, and the opera of voices pitches a key higher. Laughter is easier minute by minute, spilled with prodigality, tipped out at a cheerful word.... Dressed up in white flannels I went over to his lawn a little after seven, and wandered around rather ill at ease among swirls and eddies of people I didn't know—though here and there was a face I had noticed on the commuting train.*

A very dark undercurrent runs through the lavish gaiety of Gatsby's parties, much as it does throughout the opulence on Capitol Hill. But Amos would learn all that later (and we will advise how to steer clear of it). For now, Amos was mesmerized by what he had discovered in Washington, and he wanted another taste of it.

Amos's next great political experience would occur in Philadelphia, not Washington, in the year 2000. By now he was studying at the University of Montevallo in Alabama, and he and another friend from northeast Alabama drove to Philadelphia—nearly a fifteen-hour drive—to volunteer for the Republican National Convention. Standing outside what was then named the First Union Center doing advance work and keeping the protesters at bay seemed like a success to Amos at the time. Plus he was issued a walkie-talkie, which made him feel somewhat important.

Then, as Amos and his friend idled their time outside, a question came through the walkie-talkies asking if anyone knew how to change a tire. Apparently, no one on the outdoor crew did—except Amos and his friend. They responded to the alert, which had been issued for some VIP, and helped change the tire. As a token of thanks, the VIP gave them two floor passes to the convention.

That's how Amos found himself on the floor of the convention listening to Senator John McCain and other Republican luminaries deliver their speeches to thousands of delegates. He wasn't a senior staffer or a big-time politico then, but he had known how to change a tire and that had made all the difference. It was a night of politics that Amos would never forget.

It would be many years after the above described formative political experiences that our paths first crossed, we became friends, and eventually wrote this book together.

MAKING A DIFFERENCE

"What countries have you been to?"

The question surprised Jaime at first. He was speaking to a group of seventh and eighth graders on their first trip to Washington, DC. It was 2010 and Jaime was no longer working in the House of Representatives, where he had had a career that reached as high as the congressional leadership. As the former director of floor operations and counsel for the former House majority whip, Jaime had been responsible for the navigation and passage of key legislation and had served as a senior political and legislative advisor. In other words, he knew and worked with the most powerful members in Congress from Speaker Nancy Pelosi to Senate Majority Leader Harry Reid. He had seen history being made multiple times. And this—what countries have you been to?—was not the question he expected.

But then Jaime remembered his own first time in Washington, as a poor kid from South Carolina, and suddenly the question didn't seem so strange. These kids were also from the South, children of poor and working-class families. Many were black too. Growing up in those conditions, as Jaime well knew, can narrow a child's horizon and limit their experiences. For many, visiting Washington was the first time they had ever been on a plane. It had been the same for Jaime.

Jaime answered that he had never left the country until he worked in Congress, and since then he'd been to Singapore, Australia, Kenya, Turkey, China, and Israel, to name a few. The kids were hooked. It's likely very few of them could locate those countries on a map, but here was someone just like them who had ventured far and wide. Maybe they could too?

As they listened to Jaime tell stories of his travels and how he grew up in South Carolina, they were enthralled by how large his world had become and how similar his early life was to their own. For many, the thought of ever getting to visit other countries seemed like the greatest thing in the world.

Amos was standing in the background, and all he could do was look on and smile. A few weeks earlier, Amos had started his job as principal of a public relations firm. One of his first clients was a school that had brought a group of underprivileged students to visit Washington. It was during one of these trips in the spring of 2010 that Amos wanted to invite a speaker who could relate to the kids, particularly with their background and upbringing. Amos remembered a recent article in *Politico* that had profiled Jaime, who was by then a well-known political consultant raised by a single mother in a poor community in South Carolina.

We remembered each other from our Capitol Hill days. While Jaime worked for the House majority whip, Amos had been spokesman for the House minority whip. But our relationship didn't go much further than professional courtesy and respect. Indeed, we wouldn't speak until many years after we had both left Congress.

Now Amos needed a speaker, and Jaime seemed perfect. We should pause here to note that if Amos was simply doing his job, he would have lined up a Capitol tour and dinner at a DC restaurant. That's all the client expected. But Amos wanted to go further. He wanted to leave an impression on these young children during their first visit to their nation's capital. Like Jaime, Amos remembered his first trip to Washington as a child from the South and how the impression had remained a driving force behind his own decision to pursue a career on Capitol Hill. He really wanted to try to make the memory of these kids' first trip to Washington a lasting one.

So, years after we both had left Capitol Hill, Amos tried to get in touch with Jaime. It sounds easier than it was. In a town bursting with busy people, Jaime wasn't exactly idle. But Amos stayed after him— making calls and bugging his colleagues to ask him. Jaime was happy to oblige, but it took a phone call from Amos to explain who this group was and how important it would be for these kids to hear from him.

Neither one of us ever forgot the experience of meeting with those kids. Thus, our friendship blossomed. We always wanted to work on another project together, but life and career got in the way. Eventually Jaime left Washington and moved back to South Carolina with his wife, and where he became a father and served as the chair of the state Democratic Party and later as the associate chair and counselor of the Democratic National Committee. Amos found himself up to his eyeballs in work as partner of a prosperous public affairs firm, S-3 Public Affairs, and he was also raising three young children.

But in the back of Jaime's mind, the idea for this book began to grow. He couldn't help but wonder: how many kids might be interested in working on Capitol Hill and making a difference yet have no idea about how to get there. He saw that there weren't many resources available if you were thinking about a career on the hill, unless you already had personal connections—and how many poor kids have those? How many students across the country turn away from working in government simply because it seems beyond their means or beyond their education?

It was Jaime's wife who suggested that he find a partner for the project, preferably someone from the Republican party. Why? "Because you're always complaining about how divided politics is these days," she said. And she was right. A book from one of us would only appeal to our own side. It would likely feed the impression that to work in government one must be a partisan first, a public servant second. If that was the way it really was, neither one of us would have lasted as long as we did.

When Jaime thought about a coauthor, Amos immediately came to mind. We remembered the wonderful experience with the schoolchildren years earlier. Almost immediately the concept for the book you now hold came to us: We would write a book that, while intended for all, is targeted at those for whom Congress or their state capitol is just a place in a book or on TV, somewhere far off where only the wealthy and the privileged work. It is not; it is for you, however much money you have or wherever you live. Our government—federal, state, and local—needs people like you, and we want to help you get there.

You are probably thinking, *A job in politics? There's no way I can do that!*

Yes, you can! We did it!

Through our personal stories and the lessons we've learned along the way, we hope to convince you of that. You can work in Congress, you can work in local government, you can climb the Hill, but most importantly *you can make a difference.*

This book is not only for those looking to intern or start at an entry level in politics. We know many people who have switched careers midstream to work in politics at the state level or on Capitol Hill. This book is for them too. Young and not-so-young alike, anyone can work in politics.

EXCELLING IN POLITICS

In the United States, the ability to work in the greatest legislative body in the world is not restricted to caste or economic class. One is not born into the privilege. It doesn't matter where you live. Instead, the opportunity to work in Congress or local government is determined by an individual's intellect, work ethic, skills, and passion. We are proof of this. Starting out with little more than a dream and the will to achieve it, we both climbed the Hill almost as high as one can without receiving a vote and a congressional pin.

It is the central concept of this book that *anyone* can build a career in government, as long as one has those qualities. To work on Capitol

Hill or for your local representative is a unique honor, granted to so few throughout history. But it's not for everyone. Look at it this way: if you don't get a rush the moment you see your state capitol dome or get goose bumps on election night, a career in politics probably isn't for you.

You see, in our experience, only one type of person excels at climbing the Hill. And when we say "excel," we're not talking about who works for the most powerful member or who lands the best lobbying gig—although there are plenty of folks on the Hill and in government who do measure success that way. The only type of person who excels in climbing the Hill is the individual who contributes meaningfully to the work of the American people.

To know whether you're this type of person, it helps if you can answer this question: Why do you want to work in politics? If you're like most, your reasons probably have something to do with enjoying politics, an interest in a specific area of policy, or simply the excitement of debating the issues of the day. Believe us, those are perfectly acceptable reasons. And if those are enough to keep you going for five, ten, or twenty years, who's to say you're wrong?

Sometimes those reasons alone are not enough. There will come a day when you're making $30,000 a year answering phones or drafting the hundredth version of a form letter that you'll realize that the work is not enough. Likewise, there will come a day when you're making $100,000 advising the Speaker of the House and you won't remember why you ever wanted to participate in the Capitol Hill rat race. It happens to all staffers sooner or later.

Only staffers of a certain type can move beyond the "Capitol Hill Itch" and love their job despite the obstacles and setbacks. If you're this type, it's because you eventually remember why you wanted to work in politics in the first place: Because you want to make a difference. The people who are willing to work their way up, no matter what it takes to affect change, are the ones who truly excel in this field of work. And where better to start making a difference than in your city or state, or even in the most powerful legislative body in the world, if not in human history?

IN DEFENSE OF POLITICS

This is not to say that we or you are naive. We understand perfectly well that Congress rarely lives up to its reputation as the world's greatest deliberative body. We also know that coverage of city and state politics often revolves around the latest disgrace or political intrigue. Moreover, we know that government in general, and Congress in particular, breeds scandal, as a petri dish breeds bacteria, from the ever-titillating sexual kind to the more serious felonious and corrupt kind.

When we started writing this book, in the spring of 2012 (don't judge, we've been busy), Congress had an average disapproval rating of 75 percent. We don't want to ignore this. Anyone considering a Hill career shouldn't either. We also agree with the critics who think that Congress isn't doing what it should be doing. What you won't find in these pages is any finger-pointing. If it's fiery accusations you want, there are plenty of other books out there.

We are also aware that Washington seems to many Americans like a rather superficial and amoral place. In the summer of 2013, the big literary news was the publication of Mark Leibovich's *This Town: Two Parties and a Funeral—Plus Plenty of Valet Parking!—in America's Gilded Capital*. As a damning exposé of Washington's elite culture, the book opens in June 2008 with an account of the funeral of Tim Russert, one of the nation's top journalists and longtime host of *Meet The Press*, sadly some used it as another networking opportunity.

While Leibovich's fellow journalists take a good deal of his indignation, so do the other players in Washington's inner circle, including congressional staffers. The impression to non-Washingtonians is that this city is nothing but one big melting pot of vain, self-seeking toadies all scheming for a bigger slice of the power pie, in essence "Hollywood for Ugly People."

You can imagine what a parent reading Leibovich's book, or just surveying the Washington scene from a safe distance, would say to a child who announces: "That's where I want to work!"

Um . . . maybe you should think about medical school instead?

In any event, we would be careless if we didn't acknowledge this perception, much of which is unfortunately based in reality, head-on. We admit that one must not be canonized to work in Congress or live in Washington. We further admit that Congress often looks and acts like a three-ring circus, except with many, many more clowns. Whether on the federal or local level, power attracts the virtuous and the vain, but never in equal measure.

Nevertheless, we will defend politics as an honorable, rewarding profession despite all its imperfections. How? For starters, we worked in it and managed to escape the tempting narcissism that seems to entrap many. (We'll tell you how.) Secondly, we aren't the only ones who did. Most people who work in politics do not in any way reflect the negative image portrayed in books, cable news, or public opinion polls.

Most importantly, though, our experience working in politics taught us one of the greatest lessons in life: how to check your ego at the door and work for the greater good. It sounds trite. The simple reality is that people cannot build a successful career in government or specifically on Capitol Hill if they are egomaniacal or greedy. People like that might rise very fast, and they might meet all the right people and make all the right moves. But soon enough they will fall to earth. We've seen it happen countless times, and we'll show you how to spot them (not that they're hard to spot).

Contrary to the stereotypes, political work is a great leveler of ambition, pride, and greed. For the very reasons that it can be a frustrating place to work—a strict hierarchy, a "start at the bottom" mentality, an "I don't care where you went to school, answer those phones" ethos—it is as effective a profession for developing and improving one's character as any that exist. It's also tremendously fun and rewarding.

As we mentioned, it all depends on why you're there in the first place. If it's for the right reasons—if you deeply respect the institution, honor the opportunity, and care about your community—you'll excel as a valued employee and as a person. Those who are there for the wrong reasons are easily identified and just as easily forgotten. They'll usually take themselves out of the climb, because there comes a point when those miserable moments are simply too hard to overcome.

Which is not to say you can walk carelessly through the political world and not fear a thing. Quite the opposite, but we'll get to that later. In the end, it is possible to reach the peak of politics and remain a good person.

Our job is to show you how.

TO BE A SERVANT

You'll quickly learn whether you have skin tough enough for a political career. Despite our protestations that politics isn't all bad, it is still an industry that feasts on competition and rivalry, which can be an ugly business because democracy is an ugly business.

But the political world is also comprised of basically reasonable people doing basically reasonable things. No doubt we'll anger some people with that sentence. We know that you're coming to town to shake things up, to get those "wimps" in your party to see the way (your way) to the Promised Land. Unfortunately, that's not what the Founding Fathers had in mind—and Congress works, for better or worse, pretty much as the founders intended: that is, at a snail's pace.

This means that you will have *a lot* of time to get to know the issues and your colleagues and to represent the best interests of your district. Congressional camaraderie and civility have seen a decline as of late. Thankfully, there hasn't been a caning in Congress since 1856, when Representative Preston Brooks of South Carolina crashed his metal-topped cane upon Massachusetts Representative Charles Sumner's head. And there hasn't been a fistfight since 1902. At least compared to the ruckus that can sometimes be found in the British Parliament, Congress is generally downright tranquil.

You don't need to work on Capitol Hill for very long to see that a friendly atmosphere pervades most proceedings, whether on the House or Senate floor, or in the offices and hallways. To an American audience that sees nothing but gridlock, accusations, and finger-pointing, this might come as a shock. You'll even—gasp—make more than a few friends on the other side. This angers the partisans of both parties to no end, but there's nothing remarkable about it. If Justice Ruth Bader Ginsburg and the late Justice Antonin Scalia could be friends, and if Presidents Bill Clinton and George H.W. Bush can be friends, we're pretty sure you can make friends with your fellow staffers.

That spirit of friendship formed the foundation for this book. Before you roll your eyes and think that all we're offering is another ode to compromise, let us explain this point further. If your passion is to (metaphorically) maim, obstruct, or destroy the other side, how well do you think you're serving your constituents? Exactly. Go start a blog instead.

Let's use a word that is a bit old-fashioned these days: *servant*. To work in government is to be a servant of the people. By *people*, we're not talking in the abstract. We're talking about the actual people whom you serve and represent as a staff member to their elected representative. You're going to talk to these people; you're going to meet with them; you're going to calm their fears and raise their hopes; you're going to take their criticism and their praise in equal measure. Above all, you're going to work every day to make their lives a little better.

This is good work. It is rewarding work. It is fun, and it is hard. Believe us when we say that it is much easier to work on behalf of constituents when you can also work with your opponents.

A NOTE ON STRUCTURE

Before we get to it, we should explain briefly about the structure of this book. This book focuses on how to build a career in politics generally (including local government), with a more in-depth view of the Capitol Hill experience. Many of the lessons learned on Capitol Hill are easily transferable to other opportunities in local government. Throughout this book we use "the Hill" both literally and figuratively. Our experience as staffers was on Capitol Hill, even though Jaime went on to be chairman of the South Carolina Democratic Party. The lessons and pieces of advice we provide you stem from our tenure on the Hill. However, we also know a lot of friends and colleagues who started their careers as staffers in state legislatures and the several Hill committees. In speaking with them, we learned that our advice for the ambitious staffer applies to the state and local level as well. This book is meant to be a guide for anyone who wants to get a start in politics. "The Hill" can be your state legislature, city council, or the real one in Washington, DC. We cover state and local politics, as well as the various party committees, in more depth in chapter 6.

The first five chapters guide you through the earliest stages of Hill and political work, up to the highest levels. This is the path that we followed: We started out as interns and ended up as House leadership staff. In telling our own stories, we provide practical lessons to help you along the way. We explain the various professional paths a congressional staffer can pursue and the tactics one must use to keep climbing. While we hope our own stories are entertaining, our purpose in these chapters is to create a practical, useful reference manual that anyone can follow to build a career. As such, we focus on matters unique to the politics industry and try not to get bogged down in general "job hunting" points.

The last four chapters are less linear, more thematic. At each stage along your path up the Hill, you will be confronted with ethical and personal questions. As much as Capitol Hill is like any other office, it is also very different. Dilemmas that don't much affect employees in other professions are of critical importance to government staffers. As we've said before, politics is a messy business and you need to stay as clean as possible to keep your career on track. There are far too many otherwise good people who had to leave the Hill because of one mistake. Our aim is to answer those ethical and personal dilemmas with as much wisdom and truth as we have learned—and to do so in a way that won't scare you off!

Throughout this book we also provide firsthand accounts from our old friends and colleagues, whose experiences as staffers at various positions in federal, state, and committee positions are valuable to you. In some cases, these accounts support a lesson or point we make about political work; in others, they provide an entirely different perspective. There is no one way to climb the Hill. But we hope that you will notice a constant thread throughout their stories. Namely, that they all got into politics for the right reasons, to make a difference, and that is why they all achieved great success in their careers.

Above all, we hope to provide you with a useful guide. We're not here to score any points, so if it's dirt you want, we're sorry to disappoint. We're also not here to tell you how to cut corners or "get rich quick." If that's your aim, you don't belong in politics. Since you've picked up this book, you are probably trying to decide if you want to work in Congress or have a role in government, or maybe you have already decided that's your path. We applaud you for that decision, and now we will teach you how you can achieve your dream.

CHAPTER I

PREPARING FOR THE CLIMB

If you were going to climb a mountain, what's the first thing you would need? Probably a desire to climb the mountain. Let's face it—the rest is just details.

There are few career paths where passion plays so vital a role in one's future success as does being a politician. A clear majority of your fellow interns, should you start at the intern level, will not be back within a year. For them, a political internship is a way station, a rest stop to collect some nice work experience and preferably an even nicer recommendation before continuing their true career path. We hasten to add that there is nothing wrong with this. What you learn working as an intern in politics will serve you well throughout your life. You might decide, after spending a summer or a year in local government or in Washington, that it isn't your thing. That's perfectly okay. You've gained great work experience, good contacts, and something that's even more valuable to a young professional: You know what you *don't want to do.* Believe us, most people spend years—otherwise known as their twenties—learning what they don't want to do.

In Washington, specifically, you will also come to know some people who started as interns, believing it to be only a short gig, but caught Beltway Fever and never left. Then there are those who arrive at Capitol Hill midcareer. Most in this category don't start as interns. They usually come to Washington with a skill set that already places them in a midlevel position. We'll cover this entry point in more detail later.

However one gets to the Hill, staying on the Hill usually comes down to passion, the desire to climb the mountain. In the Introduction we chose the phrase "to make a difference" to cover the variety of interests that collectively come under this theme of passion. Indeed, each of us had somewhat different reasons for choosing a Hill career: We pursued different tracks once there, we worked for opposing parties, and we selected much different careers after we left. Nevertheless, those differences pale in comparison to our shared passion to make a difference. As it was for us, so it will be for you and your peers.

LESSON I: HAVE THE DREAM

As we explained at the beginning of this chapter, by far the most important element in building a successful career in politics is a *desire to build a career in politics*. It seems intuitive, but not when you consider how many of your peers, assuming you have yet to start your career, will *end up* in jobs they had no intention of doing. Very few people just *end up* with a successful career in politics, as if they were just going through the motions and voilà!—success.

To look at it another way, many, if not most, people tolerate their job. It pays the rent, supports the family, and leaves a little extra for recreation and savings for the future. But it's not their passion. What we can say with near certainty is that you will not like your job in politics if you don't have a passion, a dream, to be there. For many of you, this probably seems obvious. You already know you have a passion, so why are we bothering with this at all? That's great, but the point holds whether you already have the desire or simply have an interest or curiosity.

Indeed, Lesson 1 will hold throughout your entire Capitol Hill or political experience. That's why we've spent so much time discussing it. It's as simple as this.

If you don't have a desire or passion, or if you lose the desire or passion, you will not have a successful career in politics.

We don't say this to scare you off. A simple curiosity is more than enough to try out Capitol Hill or working in local government. The desire, the passion, might grow in time. Rather, we offer it as a warning that might someday save you years of grinding drudgery. To work in politics is an honor and privilege, but it is also a choice: choose wisely.

LESSON 2: TRY OUT YOUR DREAM

We decided to tell you more in our preface than you probably wanted to know about our pre-Hill youth because it is important to understand that we experienced Washington and Capitol Hill before we ever worked there. Jaime got the politics bug from watching the news with his grandfather, but he found his passion during his first trip to Washington and internships on the Hill. Amos only had to visit Washington once before his interest in politics was sparked and his ambition cemented.

For you, we advise something similar. Internships aren't necessary for a future Capitol Hill career, but they are encouraged. We both vividly remember our own first Washington experience and for that reason, you should try out your dream before diving in headfirst.

Jaime was one of a select few high school students who had the opportunity to tour Washington as part of the Hearst Foundation's United States Senate Youth Program. Amos was lucky enough to have a family friend with the contacts to secure him a highly coveted Senate internship. Getting to Washington requires curiosity, interest, and sometimes a little luck.

What we haven't mentioned yet is another experience we share: the American Legion Boys State. Both of us participated in this program as high school students, and we trace our desire to work in government and our future success to what we learned at Boys State. If you don't know about Boys State, it's an educational program of government instruction for US high school students sponsored and paid by the American Legion. Girls State is a similar program for high school girls. In these programs, participants learn about the workings of our democratic institutions and rights as franchised citizens through firsthand experiences in student-run legislatures, courts, and other assemblies.

In short, Boys State was a wonderful experience for us. That we credit the program with shaping our later careers is the greatest tribute we could give. Moreover, it's not a program that requires special access or luxurious trips to Washington. Rather, it serves as an accessible gateway to learning about a career in politics at a young age. It's like when the sought-after high school recruit visits the college campus and is given the first-class tour—only to find out much later the truth about being a freshman. In many ways, "those luxury" trips can cloud one's judgment. Boys State taught us that government work isn't all glamour and first-class hotels. It's actual work, often unheralded and away from the cameras. But we loved it nonetheless. Perhaps we would have chosen different careers had we never visited Washington, but we can say for certain that our participation in Boys State laid the groundwork for our careers on Capitol Hill.

The lesson we want to impart is that you should try out your dream before you drop everything and start knocking on Capitol Hill doors. If you don't know what you're getting into, there is a possibility you won't enjoy it. Then what? It's not the end of the world by any means. But you could have saved yourself some blood, sweat, and tears had you only learned whether you like government work in the first place.

So, as you begin to consider your first internship, check out the multitude of options that give students the chance to experience government work on an intimate scale (see Resources, page 184). We should also mention that doing this on a local level will imbue you with a sense of civic responsibility. It's a lesson we'll discuss later in this book, but you must always remember whom you're working for when in politics: It's not the media, it's not your peers, it's not even your political party. It's your constituents, who don't live in Washington, who lead ordinary lives beyond the glitz and splendor of the nation's capital.

One final point, but a particularly important one for those who work in an office building where nearly everyone is a transplant. "Don't ever be ashamed of where you're from," as a staff member for Senator Richard Shelby told Amos, no doubt because he could sense Amos's youthful unease as the high school kid from Centre, Alabama. That Amos remembers it so well almost twenty years later shows how important it was (and is) to him.

We have never been ashamed of our background. (Nor have we been overproud to the point of arrogance.) Should you embrace Washington as your new home, we hope you love it as much as we do. Yet it seems to us that one of the principal reasons Capitol Hill thrives is because it represents some of the best of America. By working there, you will bring the history, lessons, and pride of wherever you were raised to the people's house to get things done—not to mention show your fellow staffers how you do it back home.

How They Climbed the Hill
TARA DIJULIO'S STORY

I remember a moment in second grade when the teacher asked us what we wanted to be when we grew up. There were the typical answers you'd expect from seven-year-olds: astronaut, football player, ninja. When it was my turn, I didn't hesitate. "I want to be a White House reporter," I said. I don't think elementary school teachers expect such specificity from their students, because the look I got from mine was one of bewilderment. Hey, I was an odd duck.

Washington. That was my dream, a rather strange one for a kid from Southern California. But I never wavered. Throughout my childhood, through middle school and high school, I kept my sight and ambition locked on a city three thousand miles away. My family didn't help matters when we took a trip there. I fell in love. To be in the center of the political work, close to the action . . . Who wouldn't want that?

In college, I studied political science and communications. But I was still on the West Coast, at the University of Washington (Seattle), so when an opportunity for a broadcasting internship in DC came my way, I jumped at it. That's how I spent part of my senior year at the Washington bureau for Tribune Broadcasting. This wasn't your typical coffee-fetching kind of internship. They handed me a microphone and a cameraman, and told me to cover Capitol Hill. The first interview of my career was with the Speaker of the House Dennis Hastert.

The more I saw of Capitol Hill, the more I wanted to be a part of it—but not as a reporter. I made use of my alumni office to cold-call other Huskies (University of Washington folks) on the Hill, targeting press secretaries. I was shocked at how many took my call; I was even more shocked at how many agreed to sit down with me over coffee. My interest was simple: I wanted to know what their day was like as a press secretary.

After my internship, I had compiled an impressive video package, which I needed if I wanted a job in broadcasting. But I never sent in one application. I now wanted to work on the Hill as a press secretary to help shape history. Upon graduation, I moved back to California, lived with a friend, and waited tables, all the while blanketing the Hill with my resume. I might have had one or two cross-country phone interviews, but it became apparent that I couldn't expect any results unless I was in DC.

On New Year's Day in 2006, I made the plunge and moved to Washington. With just enough money for first and last month's rent, I found a job waiting tables and hit the Hill hard. I would even bring a suit with me to the restaurant in case I needed to run out quickly for an interview. But still nothing happened. Even though I had covered the Hill as an intern for Tribune Broadcasting, I lacked two essential elements for landing a job there: a good connection and Hill experience.

Eventually, I found a better-paying (and connected) gig at a lobbying firm, where I was an executive assistant. I also shifted my job-hunting tactics. I kept blasting my resume out, but I focused more on meeting anyone connected to the Hill. I was meticulous on this point. I kept an Excel spreadsheet listing everyone I met, how we met, and what we talked about. I sent handwritten thank-you notes and Christmas cards. Finally, a bite . . .

Through the lobbying firm, I connected with Senator Bob Bennett's chief of staff, who passed my resume along to the communications director, who passed it along to Senator Wayne Allard's communications director, Steve Wymer. (This is how resumes get around.) I got an interview for a deputy press secretary position under Allard. Before the meeting, I did my research and saw that Steve was a Cougar, as in Washington State University Cougar—my alma mater's big rival. It wasn't much of a connection, but it was something. The interview itself was fairly conventional and routine, until Steve asked me if I had any questions for him. I had a line in my back pocket that I planned to use only if I needed a miracle. I needed one then.

"Yes," I said, heart racing. "I never thought I'd see the day when a Husky would be begging a Cougar for a job."

Silence. A smile. Laughter.

The job was mine.

—**TARA DIJULIO,** director of public affairs, GE

CHAPTER 2

TAKING THE FIRST STEPS

"I have to do what?"

"We need you to deliver watermelons."

During Jaime's summer internship in the Senate, there was a point when he found himself delivering watermelons to other offices. It was the summer after Jaime's first year at Yale—a university one high school advisor told him to avoid. "You probably won't get in" was the curt message. Jaime got in, on a scholarship no less. He wanted to study American government and intern on Capitol Hill.

Well, he got his wish and secured an internship in the office of South Carolina Senator Fritz Hollings. It was the dream internship he had wanted since first visiting DC a year earlier. Everything seemed to be going Jaime's way.

Except now he was in a suit lugging around boxes of watermelons. Jaime thought, "What the hell? I can't believe we are delivering watermelons?!" On its face, it was a bit awkward, but there was nothing sinister or nefarious about the situation. One can actually think of it as an annual initiation of summer interns from South Carolina, since every year the South Carolina Department of Agriculture works with the South Carolina Congressional Delegation to bring fruit like watermelons or peaches to share with other members on Congress, and it falls to the congressional staff, but mainly the interns, to deliver the fruit.

Did Jaime work his butt off in high school, earn a scholarship to the one of the best universities in the country, then obtain a highly competitive internship in a top-ranking Democratic senator's office only to deliver watermelons? No, of course not. But that's what being an intern on Capitol Hill means. You answer phones; you open mail; you fetch coffee; you meet people; you network; and, occasionally, you deliver watermelons. Jaime learned early that success on Capitol Hill meant getting the job done regardless of what the job was. He also learned that little things like a giving a colleague a watermelon can go a long way in maintaining good and productive relationships.

THE INTERNSHIP, IN FOCUS

Throughout this book, we'll often return to the theme, There is no one way. As in, there is no one way to get an internship on Capitol Hill. Amos got his first internship through a family friend; Jaime by simply sending in a resume. This is not to suggest that there aren't correct and incorrect *methods* to obtaining an internship. We just want to make it clear that the methods we offer aren't the only ones.

The first question you might have is, Where do I start?

Major or Course of Study

You don't need to be a poli-sci or American government major to get an internship on Capitol Hill or at the local level. Many of you reading this likely are, so we should say that it certainly doesn't hurt. We'd only add a special warning: Answering the phones for thirty days on Capitol Hill will bring everything that you learned in those thirty hours of poli-sci course work to life. Reading about "how the sausage is made" is great, but actually seeing it take place is a very special learning experience. On-the-job training enhances and adds context to the academic knowledge you gained in school.

Now, if your major or area of interest has no literal connection with politics, don't be alarmed. During our internships, we knew English majors, biology majors, history majors, education majors, and nearly every other major under the sun. Like most companies, Congress isn't looking for the student who knows what a subcommittee does or what a markup is; they're looking for the most competent coffee getters higher education has to offer. We kid. But you get the point.

That said, you should know *something* about politics, American government, and, ideally, the senator or other Congress member for whom you want to work. In this case, it helps to be up to date on basic current events. There's a difference between knowing political history and knowing today's political climate. To be able to talk intelligently about what's happening in the world of politics *right now* will erase whatever inadequacies you might have in your academic major. In other words, read a newspaper every day so you can answer these basic questions.

What party controls Congress (or your statehouse)?

Who are the Speaker of the House, the Senate majority leader, and the minority party equivalents?

Who are your senators and representative (assuming you aren't applying for a job with either)?

What major bills, issues, and the like have been passed or debated in the last year or so (and what do you think about them)?

We hope you can answer these questions already. But you'd be surprised how many interviewees cannot when they're face-to-face with the interviewer.

Political Party

It's our experience that most college students who want to work on Capitol Hill already have strong political opinions. They know which party they want to work for and which party they want to stamp into the ground with the heel of their shoe. If we had written this book ten years ago, this is the piece of advice we would offer: don't worry so much about party when applying for internships.

We wish that were still true today, because the internship should be used to learn about the business of politics, not to enforce strict partisan divisions. Sadly, things have changed. Partisan divisions have seeped down to the lowest entry point for politics, at least in Washington. It's very unlikely in today's political climate that a southern Republican conservative would hire a former intern for a Democratic Senate firebrand. So, yes, you should carefully consider your choice of party before applying to any internships.

That said, you shouldn't treat your internship as a partisan activity. The primary purpose of your internship is to acquire Hill experience, including making friends and connections. Your work as an intern will be nearly identical whether you work for a Republican or a Democrat. Let's be honest: You're not going to be drafting legislation or devising strategy. You're going to be doing the mundane busywork that no one else wants to do. That work is fairly standard across partisan lines.

You won't be crafting partisan messages or blasting the other side with your witty tweets. You'll have to learn to leave your partisan enthusiasm at home and focus on the tasks before you. This might be difficult if your partisanship animates your desire to work in politics. If that's the case, see how well you enjoy your internship experience. You might find that the very nature of staffer work isn't for you. Perhaps you'd be better suited to a journalism or activist line of work.

Start Local

Each of our first internships was with our home-state senators. We strongly urge you to start your application process there, at the local level. Congress members usually hire interns from their home state. It's not a hard-and-fast rule, but it helps the offices weed out the applicants, of whom there are more than enough home-staters. By all means, go for the Senate internship, but don't ignore your House representative. Think about it: There are only two senators for any state. The pool of applicants therefore is statewide (if not nationwide). Just playing the odds, you have a better chance of getting an internship with your local House member. Only when you've exhausted your House members should you start to branch out nationwide, and even here, try to stick with states with which you have a connection: that is, where you grew up or where you go to school.

As you advance up the Hill, the state connection will mean less and less. But at the intern level, it means everything. If you happen to strike out with landing an internship in Congress, don't ignore the local Congressional district offices. Starting there could lead to Washington the next summer. Incredible opportunities can be had interning at your state legislature or mayor's office. The point is to open the door and get that all-important experience. A stint in your state legislature one summer will get you one step closer to obtaining that Washington internship the next summer, and will allow you to compare federal and state governments as well.

How to Apply

By far the best ways to find and apply for an internship are by contacting a senator's or representative's office directly by phone or email, or even by scheduling an appointment with the intern coordinator in a local office. Programs that work closely with congressional offices might have an inside track should you come up empty with the direct approach. Jaime's second time interning on the Hill was with the Congressional Black Caucus Foundation intern program. There are several organizations like the CBCF that provide opportunities for students, particularly those from underrepresented communities. (We list some of the better-known ones in Resources page 184.) You can also contact your college career services office or high school guidance counselor for help; many of these offices have connections in the Washington area.

In this day and age of social media, you should also start networking. Reach out to friends, family, and whomever else you know to see if they have any contacts in Congress. Websites like LinkedIn and Facebook are great tools for finding these connections. Explore these sites to locate alumni from your college or university who may be working in government. You're all but certain to find someone who can help point you in the right direction.

It's important to note that "connections" mean less at the intern level than at the staff level. This is not to say that connections can't open doors. But we don't want to leave you with the impression that you need to have an inside track to land an internship. Particularly in Congress, internships are part of an organized program, and while they are hard to get, they aren't impossible. Stick with it, exhaust your options, and you should be successful.

Internships Everywhere

If at first you're not successful, don't be discouraged. Congress isn't the only place that needs interns during the summer months. At least a hundred other organizations in town offer intern experience that would cross over well to congressional work: think tanks, campaign committees, advocacy organizations, lobbying groups, law offices, and media outlets. If you strike out in Congress, your next step is to find an internship in line with your political interests—and in Washington, if that is your ultimate goal. As for most any industry, proximity is the surest path to success. If you're in Washington working and meeting people, your chances of landing a congressional internship eventually will increase tenfold.

A CITY OF INTERNS

Every summer, an estimated twenty thousand college students and graduates arrive in Washington to begin what is for many their first real internship or job. That's seven thousand more people than live in Orangeburg and seventeen thousand more than live in Centre. In other words, a nice-sized town descends on the nation's capital for three months out of the year, an event the locals anticipate and dread in equal measure. Let's remember that the demographics of this "town" consist of young adults, full of energy, hormones, and confidence. Sometimes it can feel like spring break on the Potomac—except every weekday morning you're expected to arrive on time in business attire ready for work.

Who is there to work and who is there to party will be very apparent early on. The two characteristics that won't help you make the distinction are intelligence and ambition. Most of your fellow interns will be very smart, and most will be very ambitious. But only a few are interning in Congress because they want to stay in Congress. Seek out people who want to build a career early and form relationships with them (yes, even if you can't stand them). Relationships and networking are core ingredients in success in politics. Make those connections. Keep them. Maintain them. They will only help you later.

For now, either you're serious about making the most of your brief time interning in politics or you're not. All we can say is stay away from the twenty-four-hour partiers and make the most of the opportunities an internship has to offer.

These opportunities could be simply going to a committee hearing or sitting in on a policy briefing. Almost always these experiences will be outside your scope of work as an intern. In other words, these opportunities won't be a part of completing your daily tasks. Often, you'll have to squeeze them in before you start your workday—Washington loves breakfast sessions—during your lunch break, and after work. We don't have a set number of these extracurricular events you should attend. But you should set aside fun and games, happy hours, and yes occasionally sleep, to attend as many that interest you.

How do you know what will interest you? Let's put it this way: If you can't find something in Washington that interests you, you have no business being in Washington. There is no shortage of events on or off the Hill to satisfy whatever interest or curiosity you have. One of the marvelous gifts of Washington is that it caters to all special interests. So, go hog wild! And we don't need to stress the value of learning a thing or two at these events; meeting new people and making new friends; and talking, talking, talking to as many people as you can.

What should begin to happen if you take this part of your internship seriously—and don't waste every free minute at happy hours or recovering from happy hours—is that you'll start to understand what you want to be on Capitol Hill. Your dream of "working on Capitol Hill" will narrow down to "doing *this* on Capitol Hill."

Is policy your passion?

Then what kind of policy?

Literally dozens of policy shops and think tanks around town hold small and large events on any given night.

Is the game of politics your passion?

Is it party politics or ideological politics?

All the national parties and leading ideological organizations have sponsored events, guest speakers, book signings, and activist meetings on any given night.

You get the idea. During the summer months, the frequency of these events only increases. So, get out, find something to attend, and—above all—*don't waste your time.* Believe us, some of your internship responsibilities will likely fail to satisfy your intellect and ambition. You may sometimes even—gasp!—think you're too good for them. It can be problematic to *think* this way; it's a whole other thing to *act* this way. Go about your daily routine with a wink and a smile. Just be happy you're there. On your own time, when you're off the clock, you can explore and indulge other interests.

That said, your future success depends greatly on how you perform and act during office hours. Answering constituent phone calls, sending mail, researching issues, and even delivering watermelons are equally important tasks because *someone is always watching.*

LESSON 3: ACT AS IF SOMEONE IS ALWAYS WATCHING

Even though interns are given the office grunt work, it doesn't mean no one notices. One thing that unites congressional staffers is that nearly everyone started at the bottom. Which means that everyone knows that the person at the bottom today might be your boss tomorrow. They'll still treat you like an intern—it's part of life, unfortunately— but your superiors also know full well that many members were once interns themselves.

As an intern for Senator Hollings, Jaime wasn't old enough to drink, which gave him no choice but to miss out on office happy hours. He made up for the missed bonding time with coworkers by working extra hard during work hours. His superiors, in particular Joey Lesesne, took notice. Some years later when Lesesne became Senator Hollings's chief of staff, he would offer Jaime a position as a legislative assistant for education policy. Jaime didn't take the job, but it confirmed to him that his actions as an intern had a direct impact on his future employment prospects.

LESSON 4: THE ANSWER IS ALWAYS YES

As an intern, whenever a superior asks you to do an assignment, your answer should always be yes. Even if you have another assignment that takes priority, you still say yes, while explaining that you'll get to it right after you finish your current task. And then do the assignment to the best of your ability. Most congressional internships are unpaid, which means an intern doesn't cost the office any money. The benefit of this is that it's extremely hard to get fired (but by no means impossible) for doing something wrong. It's unlikely you'll be tasked with a job whose outcome is of vital importance. So, don't be afraid to do anything and everything that comes your way.

The flip side is that thousands of eager young people want to take your spot should you fail or become disinterested in the work. Therefore, if nothing is coming your way, ask for something to do. Amos's second experience in Washington, following his internship with Senator Shelby, was with a public relations firm. Although this was not an internship, Amos was paid less than the guy answering the phones at the reception desk. That's not a lot of money. Amos did his job and focused his efforts on how to move up within the firm.

Amos told his supervisor how he felt one day, and her response, while unsympathetic, was invaluable: She told him to start arriving early and to ask his boss for more work. It's as simple as that. *Make your-self useful. Ask for more responsibility.* Every congressional office has a list of work no one wants to do, which means you should be asking to do them. In the unlikely event that you run out of work, ask for more.

During Jaime's second summer internship as a Congressional Black Caucus Foundation intern, in the office of Representative James Clyburn, he followed the same work ethic he had learned in Hollings's office: work hard, remain diligent, and stay after hours. By following this simple formula, Jaime found himself, an intern, bonding with Clyburn's chief of staff, Yelberton "Yebbie" Watkins. That relationship led to tasks that weren't as menial as delivering watermelons. For instance, Jaime was asked to help prepare Clyburn's presentation to the Congressional Black Caucus Foundation Annual Legislative Conference. In July of that summer, it was Jaime's responsibility to write a congressional tribute to golfer Justin Leonard, remarks that Clyburn would read on the floor of the House of Representatives that summer. Although less than four hundred words, the tribute Jaime wrote and Clyburn read remains forever in the Congressional Record. Not bad for an intern.

LESSON 5: OPENING DOORS OPEN DOORS

Although it is a city infused with decorum, Washington isn't exactly known for its manners. Once again, JFK's famous line about being a city of "Northern charm and Southern efficiency." Some could say that this description could be used for some state capitals as well. An insightful intern, anxious to stand out from the crowd, might notice that if you flip JFK's idiom, you can get noticed. Which is what Amos did during his early years on the Hill. As an intern for Senator Shelby, Amos turned heads with his southern charm. He was friendly and gregarious, and he literally opened doors for others. It's a small point but it bears emphasis: You will never lose by making yourself helpful and being respectful. If you're an intern, your primary task should be to get noticed (in a good way); this means not being above opening doors, fetching coffee, running out for lunch, or any of the thousand little details that aren't necessarily your responsibility but will make someone else's day go a bit better.

When Jaime was an intern for Senator Hollings, he formed a bond with the Senator's wife, Rita "Peatsy" Hollings, over their mutual love: education. When he returned to school that fall, he began personal correspondence with her. He didn't have to write letters to her, but it was a great way to learn more about South Carolina's history of improving schools, and unknowingly it also endeared him to someone whom the senator listened to more than anyone else. Of course, that's not why Jaime did it. Nor should that be why you open the door for your chief of staff or the janitor. You do it because you're happy to serve and be helpful.

Too many congressional interns treat their summer in Washington as an internship. They aren't paid, they have no large responsibilities, and they could disappear tomorrow and few would notice. From this perspective, why shouldn't an intern enjoy his or her spring break on the Potomac? The serious intern, the one who wants to return to Congress, knows that the internship is what you make of it. It can be a party, or it can be the key that will open doors of future opportunity or slam them shut—the choice is yours.

How They Climbed the Hill
NADEAM ELSHAMI'S STORY

My first job on Capitol Hill was in the Senate mailroom. I was a college graduate with dreams of being a Hill staffer, so you might think I was a bit dispirited. You'd be wrong. I loved it. I was one of many college graduates delivering the mail to Senate offices, all of us with dreams of becoming a communications director or chief of staff one day. We also had what no one else trying to land a staffer job did: a Hill ID badge, which allowed us to walk the Capitol, meet people, and make connections. I would have my ID badge for the next twenty-five years.

I didn't stay in the mailroom. I have held nearly every position one can have as a Hill staffer. I've been an intern (twice), staff assistant, press assistant, deputy press secretary, press secretary, communications director, deputy chief of staff, and chief of staff. I worked in these roles for multiple members: representatives Bob Clement and Jan Schakowsky, senators Barbara Boxer and Dick Durbin, and, my last boss, former House Speaker Nancy Pelosi.

You could say my Hill career was marked by transitions. I moved from communications to policy (and back); I moved from the House to the Senate (and back); and I moved from the caucus to the leadership, from the leadership to the speakership (and back). Each transition, whether it was a new title or a new member, had its own learning curve, its own initial phase of discomfort and foreignness. But I enjoyed the challenge. I thrived in an environment where I had no choice but rise to the occasion. You should, too, if you want to succeed on the Hill.

Regardless of where I was or what I was doing, my goal was the same: to serve my member to the best of my ability. We all get into politics to make a difference, but one succeeds on the Hill by protecting and promoting his or her member. For me, better job titles and greater responsibilities meant I was better positioned to serve my member. My thinking: Could I help my member better as a staff assistant or as a press secretary? Could I do more for my member as a communications director or as chief of staff?

It's that sense of duty to your member that must never change, no matter how high up the Hill you climb. I first entered Nancy Pelosi's office as the deputy communications director. The moment of working for the first woman Speaker of the House wasn't lost on me. By this point, I had been on the Hill for fifteen years—I had seen and done pretty much all of it, and yet I felt like I had to learn everything again. It was a transition for everyone. At such a moment, it's easy to lose your way, to let yourself get overwhelmed. My rule during those first days working for the Speaker was to keep my head down, put up the blinders, and serve her to the best of my ability.

And that's the one piece of advice I can offer. It doesn't matter where you find yourself on the Hill, whether you're an intern or a chief of staff. You will encounter moments and episodes that seem overwhelming, either for their sheer magnitude or because the burden seems too great. During such times, keep your head, keep your blinders on, and serve your member. If you do, you will be rewarded with a rare gift, one that so few others ever see in their lives. It's the gift of being a witness to history and knowing that you played a part.

I recall sitting in Nancy Pelosi's office, as her chief of staff, when the Supreme Court decision on the constitutionality of the Affordable Care Act was read. It was an amazing moment, one that I will never forget. The very next moment I was back to work.

—**NADEAM ELSHAMI,** executive vice president,
  SIGNAL Group DC

CHAPTER 3

ESTABLISHING BASE CAMP

In February 2013, the website Amos founded, FamousDC.com, published an article about the rules to live by your first week on the Hill. We reprint most of it here because it's as fine a summary as you'll find of the essentials for all new congressional staffers (if Amos does say so himself).

1. There are reporters who have dreams about finding a member of Congress caught in a scandal. Remember this—you never know who's watching your actions. Never forget that you represent a member of Congress. Do you really want that @mail.house .gov email in the *Washington Post*? How about on Twitter or Facebook? Think twice before you hit Send (or Reply All for that matter—not always a good thing to land on the front page of *Buzzfeed*).
2. Unless you have a title of press secretary or communications director, don't spend much time chatting with reporters about the office, the member, or how he spends his time. Please refer to #1.
3. You work for someone who had MILLIONS of dollars spent against her in the primary and the general election. This also included opposition researchers. There are lots of people watching what you do as a staffer. Again, refer to #1.

4. There may be days or constituent calls that don't make it feel like such, but this is a serious job. This isn't a college fraternity. Remain professional and treat colleagues with respect and remain professional. Did we mention remain professional? Your next job in leadership or downtown will come from a meeting you have while you're in this office. We promise.

5. YOUR INTERN TODAY WILL PROBABLY BE YOUR BOSS ONE DAY. This happens all the time. Seriously. So send them for coffee only when it's a top priority.

6. Your colleagues will likely want to go out drinking. Don't be the first one there—or the last one to leave. Don't forget, there are reporters and opposition researchers who like to hang around nearby tables when certain offices get drunk and start loudly complaining about their boss, colleagues, or other offices. Again, we cannot stress #1 enough. Also, be the first one into the office the morning after a night out with the staff—or at least beat your boss into the office. (For those heavy hangover days we also suggest keeping a packet of Emergen-C in your desk along with some Advil. Have a stacked office drawer and you'll make plenty of friends with your fellow staffers.)

7. The member's spouse is more important than the chief of staff, legislative director, and communications director combined. Don't forget it.

8. Learn it, live it, love it. Working on Capitol Hill will teach you more about government than a master's degree on the subject. Soak it up.

9. You have an incredible job and one that a lot of people would love to have. Enjoy it. Everything passes through Capitol Hill: declarations of war, humanitarian aid, famous athletes, and global celebrities. We live in a great country. There are days when it won't feel like that, in which case, take a step back, go stand outside, look down the National Mall, and remember that you're living on the front lines of history.

Words to live by indeed. We're going to get into detail with many of the points above in chapter 8, where we tackle more practical concerns. For now, it's important to keep a list like this always in the forefront of your mind during your first job on the Hill.

In any case, now we get to the meat of it. Passion? Check. Internship? Check. Diploma? Check. Polished resume with no lies or laudatory letters of recommendation from people you only met once? Check. Job? Um . . . figure out how the place works first.

UNDERSTANDING HOW CAPITOL HILL OPERATES

Anyone who is considering working on the Hill has probably sat through a Political Science 101 course and picked up some basic knowledge on our legislative branch of government. You know that it is bicameral, meaning two chambers—the Senate and the House of Representatives. You know that there are 535 members—100 senators and 435 representatives. You even know some of the leaders in the Congress: the Speaker of the House, the Senate majority leader, and someone called a whip. Nonetheless, even with some basic knowledge, many Americans fail to understand how Congress and the Hill operate. Most of the actions by our representatives takes place in three spheres.

Congressional leadership, which sets the directions and strategy for Congress and each party.

Committees, which conduct hearings and investigations, and produce legislation for consideration.

Members' personal offices on the Hill and in their congressional districts, which serve as the link between citizens and their elected representatives.

As you begin to explore opportunities to work on Capitol Hill or any legislative body, it is important to understand the landscape which things get done in order to find the best place for you.

Capitol Hill: Personal Office—DC and Congressional Districts

Once elected, members of the House of Representatives and the Senate are given allowances to set up offices in Washington and district offices in their home state. Members of the House can hire up to eighteen permanent employees and four temporary employees or paid interns. Senators, however, have a larger staff and are provided allowances based on their state's population. In theory, senator offices don't have numerical restrictions or caps on the number of staff hires. It is important to understand that, despite being equally important, the functions of a member's DC office and state or district offices are different.

Members of Congress utilize their district offices to assist constituents with issues related to federal grants, programs, and benefits. For instance, if people are having issues with the Social Security Administration, they would work with staff in a member's district office. Some of the key staff roles in a district office include district director, caseworker, district scheduler, field representative, and grants/projects coordinator.

A member's DC office focuses more on policy and legislation. Staff in this office interact with constituents from the member's district on policy issues. They are also responsible for overseeing the member's committee-related work and for keeping the member updated on all legislation and policies under consideration and potential impacts on citizens and organizations within the state. Key staff roles in the Washington office include chief of staff, legislative director, communications director (and/or press secretary), scheduler, legislative assistant, legislative correspondent, and staff assistant. Because members of the Senate have more staff, it is easier for a legislative assistant in the Senate to specialize in one or two topics, whereas a legislative assistant in the House may be responsible for overseeing multiple policy areas and issues.

Capitol Hill: Committees

Committees are the legislative heart of Congress, where the most intensive focus and debate on policy take place. Each member of Congress is assigned to at least one legislative committee, and many members sit on several. Committees are allocated a budget to conduct their business and to hire staff to facilitate a committee's work. A committee traditionally has a chair or ranking member (sometimes referred to as vice chair in the Senate). Traditionally, in the House of Representatives, a committee's budget is allocated with two-thirds going to the majority party and one-third to the minority. Thus, there is a tremendous difference in staff size between the majority and minority parties. In the Senate, resources are negotiated among leadership based on majority-to-minority ratios.

Traditionally, party leaders of the committee determine and sign off on staff hiring. Each committee is different, but in general the members sometimes have input on staff hires and are even given an allocation out of committee resources to hire a designated staffer. Some of the common staff roles include staff director, chief counsel/general counsel, clerk(s), professional staff, office manager, communications director, staff assistant(s), and parliamentarians. These individuals tend to be experts in their field and policy subject area. If you have a master's or PhD, it may make sense for you to try and get on a committee's staff. In addition, committees have their own intern/fellow programs.

Capitol Hill: Leadership

If committees fuel the legislative process on the Hill, party leadership in Congress develops strategy for passage. Congressional and party leadership dictate and determine legislative schedules, policy stances, party strategy, and oversee the general operations of each chamber. For many staffers, working in a leadership office is the culmination of a successful Hill career. Therefore, garnering a leadership staff role can be extremely difficult. We were both fortunate not only to have worked in a leadership office but also to have served in leadership while being in the majority. And, yes, in the House of Representatives there is a distinct difference. In the Senate, the trappings of leadership are not dramatically different regardless of whether serving in the majority or the minority. However, the House is a body that runs on the notion of majority rules. If you are in the majority, you determine the floor schedule, resource allocations, rules, and the like. If you are in the minority, you are constantly reacting and responding to the actions of the majority.

To understand leadership is to understand the roles that comprise the leadership teams. Leadership structures in the House and the Senate and among Democrats and Republicans differ little, except for the position of Speaker of the House. Congressional leadership roles include the following.

Speaker of the House: The Speaker of the House is third in line of presidential succession and technically doesn't even have to be a member of the House of Representatives. The Speaker's role is larger than being the leader of his or her party. This person is the leader and presiding officer for all members of the House of Representatives regardless of party. The Speaker sets the tone and agenda for what Congress will consider and works with committee leadership to set the legislative agenda and items of consideration.

Majority and Minority Leaders: Each chamber has a majority leader and a minority leader (also known as majority and minority floor leaders). These individuals are selected by their respective party to serve as the lead spokesperson and strategist for how the parties operate. The majority leaders oversee scheduling bills for floor consideration and debate.

Majority and Minority Whips: The next common positions are those of majority whip and minority whip. These individuals are the chief vote counters for their respective parties and are in charge of making sure that members vote with their party on major legislative debates.

Party Caucus and Conference Chairs: The last common positions are those of party caucus chair and conference chair. Democrats meet in a group called a Democratic Caucus; Republicans label their group the Republican Conference. The role of the caucus or conference chair is to preside over the weekly member meetings and the work done in caucus or conference meetings. The work can include leadership elections, ratification of committee appointments, and determining the party's stance on a major issue.

Leadership members each receive a budget to hire staff to help carry out their duties and responsibilities. Therefore, some staff types may be unique to the specific role of a leadership office, but some common roles are found across leadership offices. These include chief of staff, communications director/press secretary, policy director/advisor, member services coordinator, floor director/assistant, outreach director, director of scheduling, counsel, and staff assistant. Leadership offices also have their own internship programs.

COMMON ROLES FOUND IN
CAPITOL HILL OFFICES

PERSONAL— DC OFFICE	PERSONAL— DISTRICT OFFICE	COMMITTEE	LEADERSHIP
Chief of Staff/ Administrative Assistant	District Director	Staff Director	Chief of Staff
Legislative Director	Caseworker	Chief Counsel/ General Counsel	Policy Director/ Advisor/Counsel
Communications Director/ Press Secretary	District Scheduler	Communications Director/Press Secretary	Communications Director/Press Secretary
Scheduler	Field Representative	Clerk	Member Services Coordinator
Legislative Assistant	Grants/Projects Coordinator	Professional Staff	Floor Director/ Assistant
Legislative Correspondent		Office Manager	Press Secretary
Staff Assistant		Staff Assistant	Outreach Director
Office Manager		Parliamentarian	Director of Scheduling

UNDERSTANDING LOCAL GOVERNMENT: GOVERNORS, LEGISLATORS, MAYORS, AND COUNCILS

One of the reasons American democracy works is because its practice and ethos permeate all levels of our country. This doesn't mean that a mayor's office works exactly like Congress or that state legislatures look the same in fifty states. The peculiarities of these variant forms of American democracy are what gives this country its unique civic flavor, quite unlike almost anything you'll see in the world. In many ways, the United States as a country began at the local level, with many town assemblies, councils, state legislatures, and governors' mansions claiming an older heritage than the federal government. Many of these communities are fascinating in that they have developed their distinct brand of American democracy.

Which is another way to say that we can't possibly list all the things you'll need to know if you want to start at the state or local level. There are thousands of towns, cities, and counties across this great land, each one with a governing structure similar to but also very different from any other. Likewise, the fifty state legislatures and governors' offices all resemble each other (and their counterparts in Washington, DC): They all have the traditional legislative, judicial, and executive branches. But any DC politicos who think they're going to waltz into Montgomery, AL, or Columbia, SC, and run the place will quickly learn the error of their ways.

Yet there are some broad insights we can make to help get you started on exploring these bountiful, quirky, and exemplary forms of American democracy.

Governors

Like the president, a governor is the chief executive, but of the state government. (The powers of the various governors vary greatly, depending on each state's constitution.) In addition to overseeing the administration of state law, governors have the authority to appoint individuals to oversee or serve as members of state agencies, committees, councils, and the like. They also have the responsibility of mobilizing the state's military and emergency personnel, much as the president is the commander in chief of America's armed forces. For example, when a natural disaster strikes, a state governor is almost always the official in charge of any relief efforts (for which the federal government might provide funding and personnel).

The size of a governor's staff depends greatly on the size of the state. Larger states tend to have larger governor's offices. Some states have hundreds of staff; others have tens of staff. According to a 2006 National Governors Association survey, the average governor's staff size is approximately sixty-five professional and administrative employees.

General areas of operations found in the governor's office include communications/media; legal counsel; policy/legislative; political; external relations/community outreach; office of first spouse/residence; intergovernmental/cabinet/agency affairs; scheduling; advance; emergency planning; and Washington, DC, liaison (more on this below).

Common positions in a governor's office (mirroring the positions you find at the federal level) include chief of staff and deputy chief of staff; executive assistant; director of scheduling and advance; legal counsel; policy/legislative director; political director; staff of first spouse; director of Washington, DC, office; and communications/press director.

Most people don't know that every state executive office either maintains a DC office or has hired consultants who serve as liaisons to Washington and Congress. This unique role affords an opportunity to operate in both federal and state legislative worlds, and speaks to the close association of the governor's office with the White House and congressional activities. Governors wield a lot of power in Washington (as evidenced by the sheer number who have gone on to become president), and their voices are heeded in the West Wing and halls of Congress.

Legislatures

Nearly every state follows federal precedent and has a bicameral (two-chamber) legislature. (Nebraska is unicameral.) In most states, the upper chamber is called the Senate. The lower chamber doesn't hew so closely to the congressional model. Virginia's lower chamber, for example, is called the House of Delegates; many states call theirs an assembly. Despite the similarity in structure, there are some stark differences in how state legislatures operate.

Congress operates on a full-time basis, and its members are paid full-time salaries and have larger staffs. However, most state legislatures are "in session" for three to six months, and most state legislators (and their staff) are paid on a part-time basis. The part-time nature of the legislatures dramatically impacts the number of staff and the scope of their work.

Certain state leadership roles are functionally the same as their congressional counterparts but operate very differently. For example, the Speaker of the House is a powerful position in Congress and has significant influence over the operations of the legislative branch. However, the role of Speaker may be even more powerful in some state legislatures. In the US House of Representatives, each political party assigns its own members to committee slots and makes appointments. In some state legislatures, the Speaker has sole responsibility for making committee assignments regardless of whether the Speaker is of the same party as the assigned member. This feature weakens the power of the parties to provide incentives for good behavior and party loyalty, while providing the Speaker with more influence and tools to cut individual deals.

It is important to note that with fewer staff, members in state legislatures must share staff. This odd situation means that you, as a state staffer, may not be an exclusive staffer for a particular member or a particular party. But state legislative work is focused less on member and party priorities and more on the nuts and bolts of governing and getting stuff done.

Mayors and Councils

Most American cities have one of two forms of government: mayor-council or council-administrator. Based on the municipal charter, the type of government dictates the authority of the mayor and the structure of the mayor's office.

The mayor-council form of government allows for the concept of the strong mayor. American history is alive with powerful, charismatic, and sometimes corrupt "big-city mayors" who thrived from the late nineteenth century through the mid-twentieth century. Nevertheless, even in twenty-first century America, strong mayors wield a considerable amount of power. A strong mayor oversees the daily operations of the city, can veto actions by the council, and serves as the city's chief executive. Strong mayors also have the power to hire and fire personnel across city operations. Because the mayor is overseeing all city operations, the mayor's staff would likely be more expansive and include the following roles: chief of staff, director of scheduling, director of policy/research, director of communications, various department heads (community development, parks, utilities, police, fire, and so on), and director of community/external relations.

Most "weak" mayors are found in the council-administrator structure, where the mayor is a member of the council with one vote and no veto authority. The council is the real power and often holds both legislative and executive authorities. It normally hires an administrator to run the day-to-day functions and oversee the personnel and departments of the city. This office is unelected—and therefore without great political power. Mayors in this structure would likely hire a small staff to handle the ceremonial and council-related responsibilities of the office.

Regardless of the local system, the main difference between the federal bodies and their state and city counterparts is that the latter is much more focused on day-to-day governing. By this we mean that grandstanding politics has to take a backseat to making sure the "trains run on time," education is funded, and there are roads to drive on. At the federal level, we're thankful we leave these details to the states and municipalities . . . and yet, we do lose something by focusing on the "big issues." The way things get done at the local level is truly a study in politicking. It's fascinating stuff, even if it often doesn't make the front pages. If you want to learn how to make a deal that leads to results, local is your game.

ACQUIRING THE JOB

After college, Amos was hired by a public relations firm. He occupied the lowest level on the professional rung and wanted to escape. (He can safely write these things now but would never have dreamed of it back then.) In hindsight, though, PR was a good first gig for Amos, who would go on to become a communications executive.

Every day, dozens of times a day, Amos would pick up the phone and call a member of the media to pitch his clients' stories. There are few more brutal acts in the professional world that force you to continually swallow your own pride than cold-calling. But after a while, you stop taking the hang-ups, rejections, and the occasional tantrum so personally. You're just doing your job after all.

It's our experience that most recent graduates are terrified of the telephone. Believe us—we get it. It's not that it's hard; it's that the phone feels like a ten-ton weight. Yet the sooner you get comfortable cold-calling, the better.

Although Amos learned some valuable lessons working the phones at the PR firm, he hungered to get back to politics, specifically Capitol Hill. The paradox of many political jobs on Capitol Hill is that you can't work there unless you have prior experience. Internships certainly help, and if you have one right after college, all the better for you. You're already in the office, doing work. It's not that hard of a sell to move into a paying gig—but by no means is it guaranteed.

For Amos, and we imagine for a lot of you, there was a pretty big gap between his internship as a high school senior and when he started reaching out to the legislative offices again—more than five years to be precise. That's an eternity. All the old connections Amos thought he had weren't enough. Nothing seemed to work.

Then he took a chance. A friend was attending a going-away party for someone who was working at the House Energy and Commerce Committee. That suggested to Amos there was a job opening on the committee. He didn't know that for a fact; heck, he didn't even know anyone at the party. But he took a chance and tagged along (*crashed* might be the more appropriate word). It was the decision that changed his career.

At the party, Amos met the committee's hiring manager. When he saw her getting up to grab another round of drinks, Amos sprung to action. That was his in. He spoke to her a bit later and discovered that there was an opening for a staff assistant. Amos had no idea what a staff assistant on the Energy and Commerce Committee did, but he responded that he was interested.

"Do you mind if I give you a call tomorrow morning?" he asked.

"Sure," she replied. "Here's my card."

Amos called at 8 a.m. He got an interview and got the job.

We can't tell you exactly how to get a job on Capitol Hill. Even Amos, who had more connections than your average college graduate, found it to be a long, trying process. However, a few things about Amos's story are representative of the political job search overall.

Utilize All Sources to Find Job Opportunities

There are several websites and search engines listed in the resources that you can use for the early stages of your job search. One of the best government job sites is Tom Manatos Jobs. Tom and Jaime worked together in House Democratic leadership, and even then Tom was a wealth of knowledge and a valuable resource for aspiring Hill staffers and interns. Since then, he has helped thousands of people find government and political jobs. Utilize search engines and sites like Tom's to begin to get a sense of what is available: www.tommanatosjobs.com.

Live in the City Where You Want the Job

There simply is no better way to get a political job on Capitol Hill, in a governor's office, or in the state legislature than to already live in the city where the job is located. As with internships, sometimes the best career move you can make is to take a job, any job, in that city. Being in the city will expand your opportunities tenfold. You will meet other political staffers at bars; you will hear about openings before they spread like wildfire through the well-worn online sites; and you will be able to meet face-to-face the people you need to meet. Amos's story of landing a job after attending a party happens *every single day* in Washington and across the country. And you can't attend the party or reception if you're not there.

Take the Opportunity

If you're lucky enough, you can pick and choose which job you want in government. (We'll get more into the different jobs later in this chapter.) But most of us aren't that lucky. For example, Amos had no idea what it meant to work on a House committee, much less the Energy and Commerce Committee. His previous Hill experience was in a senator's office, and he knew he wanted to go into communications of some sort. But when the opportunity presented itself, Amos took it and didn't worry about whether it fit with his interests and career goals. It's one reason we stress again and again that you must have a passion to work in government and be in politics—all else being of secondary importance. Simply waiting for your dream job will likely mean you'll never get it.

Be Fearless

We can't tell you how often we hear stories of people finding jobs because they asked a simple question: "Are you hiring?" That's all Amos asked that night. One thing working in your favor is that in politics a happy hour, fund-raiser, golf tournament, or coffee is never just that. *Everything* is a networking or job-hunting opportunity. But only if you make it one. How to do that? Be fearless and ask. In politics, striking up a conversation with a total stranger can be the key to identifying opportunities.

Be Courteous

It should go without saying, but we'll qualify that last point with this one: be fearless, but be courteous. We can't teach you how to be a charming person at a social event. All we can say is that rudeness or transparent social/job climbing is frowned upon. Blundering your way into a conversation with someone new won't get you very far. The good news is that few will ever turn down a cup of coffee, so that's an easy place to start.

Always Follow Up

Here's a secret not unique to government: finding a new person to hire is a pain in the behind. It's why having an "in" is so valued with any job hunt. Employers would much rather hire the candidate recommended by someone they know and trust than pick blindly. Likewise, employers will almost always go for the path of least resistance in their hiring process. In practice, this means that instead of wading through a few hundred applications, the hiring manager will almost always choose the friend of a friend—or, in Amos's case, the guy she met at the party the night before. At least, she'll give that guy a chance, but only *if he calls like he said he would.* That's why Amos called exactly at 8 a.m., when the office opened. You never know who's going to supplant you as the person "top of mind" in the hiring manager's head. Maybe she met someone else at the party who seemed like a good fit for the job. But maybe that person didn't call until 9 a.m. or the following day. You see what we mean? When you say you're going to call the next day, call the next day at the earliest possible time you can call.

All of this is not to say that you can't find a job in government the old-fashioned way: looking in the want ads, sending in a resume, and hoping for the best. You should be doing that anyway. Send your resume to every job opening that looks good, but keep in mind that job openings get *hundreds* of applicants, so finding a way to stand out from the other applicants is critical. In the Resources, page 184, we list sites you should be checking every day if you're in the job hunt.

Now we're going to throw a few important caveats your way to make things a little more interesting.

LESSON 6: YOU MUST CHOOSE A PARTY

Here's the cold truth: It's almost impossible to switch parties on Capitol Hill or in most political jobs. We hate saying that because it seems to emphasize party affiliation over all else. What have we been hammering into your head? Leave partisanship at the door and be of service to others, right? While we firmly believe that remains the bedrock of any successful Hill career, we can't ignore the harsh reality.

The party you work for in your first job likely will be the only party you will ever work for in politics and government.

The only—we repeat, only—exception to this rule is if your boss, representative, or senator switches parties. (Party switching has been more frequent in state politics than on the federal level.) Then, you might be able to switch sides, but only for a short while. If, for instance, your boss switches parties and you can't work for that party, quit immediately. The longer you stay with your party-hopping boss, the harder it will be to come back to your old party. If you stick with your boss, all we can say is that we hope you enjoy the new party. The old one likely will not take you back.

It's more than likely that you already have a preferred party. There are very few people who look for a job in politics and don't identify with at least one of the parties. If that's the case, you probably have very little to worry about. We'd only advise that you make your decision as fully informed as you can. No party espouses the views of all its members. You probably have a few issues on which you disagree with your chosen party. There will probably be times when your boss asks you to fight for an issue on which you vehemently disagree. So, ask yourself whether you would be able to do that. Can you take the one issue on which you most disagree with your party and work as if you did agree?

If you can't, you need to think twice either about working in politics or about your preferred party. This is why we tell you to choose wisely. Be as informed on the issues as you can be. Find out for yourself what you think about them. Listing your issues in terms of priorities will help you here. Believe us when we say that there will come a day when you have to do something you firmly don't want to do for ideological reasons. Looking at your list of priority issues will help you overcome that ethical dilemma. Discussing your dilemma with friends, a mentor, or senior colleagues may also help you develop a game plan to resolve the issue.

But also understand that in some scenarios only two options are open for you if you have a serious objection to a given issue: ignore it and do your job, or quit. And by quit, we mean leave. The other party may not take you and depending upon circumstances it may be difficult to get hired by another member.

We aren't saying that it's wrong to quit. We're advising you to think through your decision first. If you've already done that hard thinking, if you've honestly weighed the issues and your views, you shouldn't have a problem picking the right party. Nor is it likely that you'll find yourself in such an ethical dilemma that quitting is a justifiable option. In our experience, the ethical dilemmas that usually justify quitting are of the more personal sort, but we'll get to those later.

This rule also poses problems for your job hunt. Didn't we say to take the first opportunity? We did, and now we've qualified it with this: *but only if it's with your chosen party.*

Fortunately, we have rarely seen someone who has chosen poorly. Political government positions have a way of molding one's beliefs into more practical beliefs. By this we mean that you can usually overcome ethical dilemmas based on the issues by understanding that this is but one small incident in a much larger world. Besides, politics isn't pure.

Politics involves compromise. Politics is constituent services. Politics is being around after the next election. Politics is living to fight another day. So, pick your party, pick wisely, and work to fight another day.

CAMPAIGN ACTIVITIES WHILE WORKING IN GOVERNMENT

For elected officials, the line between campaign activity and official activity can sometimes become blurred. The separation between the two worlds can be especially difficult for some government employees, particularly those who directly report to and work with the elected officials. Can government employees work on campaign-related activities? It depends. There are contributing factors that come to bear, such as the branch of government; the type of activity; and when and where the activity is taking place. This can be particularly frustrating and confusing when you are a staffer and the job is contingent upon the elected official being reelected. Let's briefly explore the various answers to this all-important question.

Congressional Staff

No federal statutes prohibit congressional employees from participating in campaign and political activity. However, ethics guidelines in the House of Representatives and the Senate provide guidance to members of Congress and their staffs on permitted and prohibited conduct. First, no official resources can be used for campaign and political purposes. What resources? Well, in this instance, resources include facilities, funds, equipment, and, yes, congressional staff time. This does not mean that congressional staff cannot engage in campaign activities; it means they are free to participate during their own time, which includes vacation, before/after work, lunch, annual leave, and the like. Staff may volunteer their time or be compensated (within certain restrictions based on seniority) for working on campaigns. However, staff are prohibited from contributing financially to the campaign of the member that they work for. Staff are not prohibited from running for state and local office, but face some restrictions, particularly if the staff member is considering running for Congress.

It is important for congressional staff to review and understand permissible activities as defined in the ethics guidelines provided by the House and the Senate.

Federal (not Congressional Staff), State, and Local Government Employees

The political activity of federal and some state, local, and DC government employees is restricted by the Hatch Act. The Hatch Act is a federal law passed in 1939 (and updated in 2012) to limit partisan influence over aspects of federal and state (executive) government. Guidance from the US Office of the Special Counsel states, "Generally, federal employees, unless further restricted, may actively participate in political management and political campaigns. Accordingly, these employees may engage in 'political activity' on behalf of a political party or partisan political group (collectively referred to as 'partisan groups') or candidate in a partisan election as long as it is not on duty or in the workplace. Political activity refers to any activity directed at the success or failure of a partisan group or candidate in a partisan election."

Some of the activities that are *prohibited* by federal employees include:

- Being candidates in partisan elections

- Using official title/authority to influence an election or participate in political activity

- Soliciting, accepting, or receiving political contributions (including hosting or inviting to political fund-raisers) with some exceptions

- Engaging in political activity while on duty, in uniform, or using government property

Some examples of political activities that are *allowed* include:

- Registering and voting in elections

- Assisting in voter registration efforts

- Contributing money to political organizations and candidates

- Attending fund-raising events

- Campaigning for or against candidates in partisan elections

- Holding office in political clubs or parties

- Volunteering to work on a partisan political campaign

The Hatch Act extends to state, local, and DC government employees who work with programs supported in whole or in part by loans or grants from the federal government. Exemptions to the act on a state level include governor/lieutenant governor, mayor, elected head of an executive department, and someone holding public elective office. In 2012, Congress passed the Hatch Modernization Act, which relaxed the prohibition of local and state government employees becoming a candidate in partisan elections as long as the employee's salary is not paid for entirely by federal funds. In addition to the Hatch Act, states and localities may have other laws and regulations that may impact the political behavior of government employees.

As we've stressed repeatedly, as a staffer or government employee you can have a tremendous amount of influence and power—the very things that others, on the outside, would want to use to their advantage. The ethics rules, as well as the Hatch Act, provide good, solid guideposts that should keep you on the straight and narrow path. But you should also use your common sense: If something sounds fishy or unethical, it probably is. Avoid it. The temptation to advance your own career or interests will be strong, but never forget that the other side is always on the lookout for any advantage to bring shame and humiliation to its opponents. Don't give the other side that opportunity. Better yet, be honest, be good, be a servant—and you'll be fine.

LESSON 7: YOU MUST CHOOSE A SPECIALTY

On page 194, you'll find a flow chart of Hill positions. This was also published in Amos's website, FamousDC.com, and like the list that started this chapter, it was meant to be tongue-in-cheek. But it also raises another important rule for you to know. First, let's give a little bit of background.

On the Hill and in some state legislatures, there are three "career paths" from which to choose. Each focuses on a different, but equally important, responsibility of any member's office. The paths all overlap to some degree, particularly at the entry-level positions, but (ideally) no one is more important than the other. (We'll elaborate in the next chapter.) The following are the specialties.

Communications

As the name says, staffers in the communications office handle all the member's internal and external communications needs, including constituent outreach, media relations, public statements, press releases, and office mail. These are the basic responsibilities for anyone starting out in the communications department. One of the first jobs in this path is **staff assistant (SA).** An SA's duties aren't limited to communications, and this position can be an entrée to policy-oriented roles as well. The following description is excerpted from the Congressional Management Foundation (CMF), which has general descriptions for all Hill positions.

SUMMARY:
The staff assistant greets visitors, answers the telephone, and answers constituent requests for general information, tours, and other inquiries. This position also monitors delivery and pickup of materials, maintains the front office, and assists with various administrative and legislative duties.

ESSENTIAL JOB FUNCTIONS:

- Answers and screens telephone calls for the Congress member and other staff members, and takes messages when appropriate

- Greets and screens visitors

- Provides staff-led tours of the Capitol for constituents and other guests

- Assists persons who have appointments with the Congress member or the staff, and works closely with the Congress member's scheduler to ensure that the member's appointments are on time and that the scheduler is aware of the visitor's arrival

- Answers constituent mail and email in both forms and individual responses in coordination with the legislative staff and the office systems manager

- Responds to constituent requests for information

- Ensures that requests for assistance are directed to the appropriate staff member in a timely manner

- Documents visitor opinions on issues communicated via telephone, including full name, address, and all relevant information as appropriate

Higher-level jobs in the communications path include **press assistant, new media director, press secretary,** and **communications director.** For your purposes, think of communications as the public face of your boss. How your boss is covered in the press; how he or she handles constituent concerns; and how he or she speaks and writes publicly are all in the wheelhouse of the communications department. Because in many cases "image" is its purview, this department handles much of the day-to-day battle that is Hill politics.

Policy

The policy department handles most of the legislative duties of the member, from issue research to briefs to casting votes. In addition to staff assistant, another entry-level job in this path is **legislative correspondent (LC).** Although the names differ, an LC and an SA perform very similar, entry-level responsibilities, with a slightly different emphasis. The CMF has the same description for both SA and LC, but we left out some purely LC duties in the SA description. Those include:

- Tracks legislation through the committee, House floor, Senate, and conference committee processes in assigned issue areas, and briefs the Congress member

- Together with the legislative staff acts as a liaison with constituents, interest groups, and committee and agency staffs in assigned issue areas

As you can see, an LC is much more involved in the member's research and legislative process. Instead of writing up the press release, the LC does the research that might go into the press release. The LC has a far greater grasp of what's happening on the floor, that is, what votes are scheduled, committee hearings, and the like. The policy department also puts together the briefs, questions, and other useful information for the member's events, such as committee hearings, panels, and public appearances. There's still politics at play on the policy side, but you won't have much of a role in contributing to the politics. You will, however, learn how to draft legislation and become an expert on a variety of issues.

Higher-level jobs in the policy path include **legislative assistant, legislative director,** and **policy advisor.**

Scheduler

The scheduler handles the member's daily itinerary, travel, and appointments. The scheduler always knows where the member is or should be, and usually knows what materials or information a member may need for a briefing, hearing, or the like. The scheduler coordinates with the staff to make sure the member is always prepared and aware of situational requirements. Here's the CMF's description.

SUMMARY:

The scheduler/executive assistant maintains the Congress member's official schedule, travel plans, and related records. This position also acts as a liaison for the member with the staff, public, and other members of Congress.

ESSENTIAL JOB FUNCTIONS:

- Prepares the daily schedule for the Congress member and distributes copies to the Washington, DC, and district offices

- Prepares detailed itineraries for the Congress member, including important numbers, locations, and contact names

- Briefs the Congress member on all scheduling activities and requests of the Washington, DC, and district offices

- Schedules all staff meetings and briefings involving the Congress member

- Coordinates scheduling of press, interviews, radio, and television time with the press secretary

- Makes reservations for the Congress member's air travel, ground transportation, and lodging

- Reviews the Congress member's mail and invitations

- Ensures that the Congress member is provided with briefing materials for each event by coordinating with event participants and the appropriate legislative and/or district staff

- Monitors the Congress member's incoming telephone calls, takes messages, and returns calls as requested

- Acts as a liaison between the Congress member and other members, committee staff, White House, and government offices and agencies to arrange for the Congress member's attendance at meetings or to coordinate travel plans

It's not a simple job, by any means. Basically, you're about as close to the member as you can possibly be throughout the day.

Unfortunately, there isn't much of a "path" in the scheduler route, a wrinkle we'll explain in a bit. Which is not to say that there isn't any opportunity for advancement. Usually the first person the member brings along to higher offices is his or her scheduler.

Now here's the real rule: Like the party you choose, the path you choose is very hard to leave. It's not impossible, which is a key difference from choosing your party. Particularly in those entry-level jobs, like SA and LC, there is enough overlap between them that picking one doesn't automatically exclude you from the other path. But the higher you go along a particular path, the harder it becomes to leave. You will reach a point when you won't be able to switch.

Don't let this scare you. Unlike the party you choose, you probably don't know which path you'll prefer until you try it. That's what the SA and LC positions are for. They help you build a foundation to begin to focus on one of the paths, and you do enough of everything that you will quickly decide what you like best. Also, if your ultimate goal is chief of staff, either policy or communications will get you there. It all depends on the member (and other factors we will get into later). So, again, don't fret too much. If you think you want to go into policy, but an SA is only job available, take it. And vice versa for communications.

Now for the bad news. For whatever reason, it is incredibly difficult to jump to another career path if you started out as a scheduler. We've seen many schedulers try to switch only to meet with extreme frustration. Now, there are always exceptions, but if the only available job is scheduler, you should know and fully appreciate this reality.

But here's the good news for the scheduler: You are one of the most powerful people in the office, because you are essentially the gatekeeper to the member and sometimes the staff as well. No one gets to your boss except through you. Washington is a town divided by access: Either you have access or you don't. The person who controls that access is the scheduler. As we mentioned, another advantage is that the scheduler is usually the first person to go with his or her boss to a higher office. That's because the scheduler knows the member better than anyone else in the office, except for the chief of staff.

That's about all we have to offer on the scheduler. Throughout the rest of this book, you'll get perspectives from the communications or policy departments. That's because Amos pursued the communications path, and Jaime the policy path. Chances are you'll choose one of those two paths, as well, if not simply because more of these positions are available, then because very few people have the skills and/or patience to be a scheduler.

HOUSE OR SENATE?

Finally, let's talk about the two chambers. What's the difference? Where should you start? Is one better than the other?

These questions have a simple answer: If you're starting out, focus on the House of Representatives. That's not only because we did but also because our example is (ahem) representative of most career staffers. We want to point out that this isn't a rule. You don't have to start in the House. We simply recommend it for a variety of reasons.

For starters, each House office is like a small start-up company, in that there are many more opportunities to distinguish yourself. Senate offices are much larger than House offices, which might give you the impression that there are more opportunities. But you're a small fish in a big pond. Moreover, in the House you have a much more intimate relationship with your boss, who's one of out of 435 representatives rather than one out of 100. For this reason, House members are closely connected to their districts as well, which has the advantage of giving House staffers a sense of accomplishment and success.

Perhaps the most important reason to start in the House is because you'll gain so much more experience. Because the offices are smaller, House staffers share responsibilities a lot. Everyone is required to wear multiple hats, as they say. And as the new kid on the block—we mean staffer—you'll be asked to do a lot. It won't be busywork. You'll be doing real Capitol Hill stuff right out of the gate. In the Senate, which has more resources and more staff, staff portfolios are much more focused on one or two defined areas.

A House office reflects House culture: fast paced, fun, and exciting. Bills begin in the House and die in the Senate for a reason. Whereas in the Senate you'd be lucky if your senator knows you at all, in the House you'll be on first-name basis with your member. (Note: Do not call a member of Congress by their first name unless they give you permission to do so; and even then, don't do it.) You'll be asked your opinion. You'll be an instrumental part in the office's success. Few jobs provide that kind of real-time action and satisfaction. More than anything else, you'll feel like you're part of a team.

Frankly, it is sometimes easier and quicker to climb to the highest echelons of Capitol Hill through the House rather than the Senate. For instance, the average age of a legislative assistant in the Senate is around thirty-two, in contrast the average of an LA in the House, which is twenty-eight. The tenure for Senate staffers also tends to be longer in positions than it is for House staffers.

The Senate isn't exactly the opposite. But as an entry-level staffer, you may do less, know less, and feel less important. Although the Senate is the "upper chamber," those sorts of distinctions don't mean much when you're starting out. Whatever "prestige" you get by working in the Senate, you lose valuable experience and on-the-job training that you'd otherwise get in the House.

We repeat: This isn't a rule. If a Senate job comes your way, take it. But if you have the choice, or if you don't know where to begin, start in the House. You'll be happy you did.

How They Climbed the Hill

JENNIFER ZUCCARELLI'S STORY

Since high school, I had always wanted to be a journalist. I studied journalism at Syracuse and thought I would get my start in the industry working at the metro desk of a midsized newspaper. My student loan debt, combined with the starting salary of a reporter, dispelled these childhood dreams. But I still loved media and needed to use my journalism degree for something. I suppose my interest in public policy, much more so than pure politics, led me to consider becoming a press secretary. But where to start? I was finishing my junior year and had no clear plan for what I was going to do after I graduated.

Washington, DC, seemed like the obvious place to begin my search, but I had zero connections there. I didn't come from what you would call an "in-the-loop" political family. My grandparents were Italian immigrants, and my father followed my grandfather into the steel industry. When I was growing up, we were comfortably middle-class, but I never knew anyone from my town who worked in Congress. However, my sister mentioned a friend of hers whose husband worked in Washington, which is when I first heard about Tony Fratto.

Through my sister's connection, I found myself on the phone with Tony, who was then a director at the US Treasury Department. I only realized it was a job interview when Tony offered me an internship. Thus, I learned my first lesson about Washington networking: Treat every conversation like an interview. I gladly accepted his offer and spent the summer before my senior year answering phones at the Treasury Department.

At least that's what I was hired to do, and I did it well. I made a point of coming in early and staying late if there was work to do. To make ends meet, I worked at a Ben & Jerry's at night and on the weekends. When I left DC, I had a Rolodex full of useful contacts. Finally, I had some sense of direction. I wanted to work in Washington, preferably on Capitol Hill.

Throughout my senior year I maintained contact with my old Treasury friends. Just an email here and there updating them on my life, asking about theirs, casually asking whether they had a job for me. (They didn't.) Did all my networking pay off upon graduation? Er, no. I left Syracuse without a job. But I moved to Washington anyway. Having spent the previous summer barely scraping by, I knew it could be done, at least for a few months. I also knew that if I was serious about working on the Hill, I had to be close to the Hill. So I found a group house in Mt. Pleasant and hit the pavement.

Within two months, I had accepted an offer at a communications firm—and it was because of someone I had met while at Treasury. It wasn't Capitol Hill, but by then I realized that if I wanted to be a press secretary, I needed some actual communication experience. The firm gave me that, but I needed more. In 2004, I volunteered for the National Republican Congressional Committee for the upcoming election.

I went in at night and made phone calls. I also traveled to Pennsylvania to knock on doors. It wasn't glamorous work, but it brought me to the attention of all the right people.

In this case, the "right person" was someone who gave me a tip on a press secretary position at the House Committee on Natural Resources. It was January 2005 and I was on the Hill.

—**JENNIFER ZUCCARELLI,** head of EMEA Communications,
  J.P. Morgan

CHAPTER 4

TRAVERSING UP THE HILL

In the summer of 2011, *National Journal* released a survey of three hundred top-level congressional staffers for its special "Hill People" issue. While the very term *top level* suggests a distorted cross section of Capitol Hill, the survey nevertheless provides a useful overview of Hill demographics.

As it relates to employee demographics in local government, Todd Gardner from the Center for Economic Studies at the US Census Bureau released a study in 2013 titled "The Racial and Ethnic Composition of Local Government Employees in Large Metro Areas, 1960–2010." This report's results are similar to those of the *National Journal* survey.

These studies raise some important questions—questions that no doubt many of you have been waiting patiently for us to answer.

But first some interesting nuggets.

It Has Been a Man's World, but That Desperately Needs to Change

Sixty-eight percent of senior congressional staffers are male. As this represents the "top level," it also suggests that the higher one climbs, the more men dominate the profession. Our own careers support this finding. Congressional staff needs greater gender parity, and the trend line indicates improvement. More women are needed in politics and

Congressional leadership. It is not good enough to have elected the first woman speaker of the House when there is not a defined path for other women to achieve similarly. Women face obstacles in state government as well. For example, in South Carolina women hold 15 percent of the seats in the state legislature, despite being 51 percent of the state population. Until recently, no women served in the forty-six member South Carolina senate. It is important to understand the current reality of women in politics and for all of us to continue to push for equal representation and to change the male-dominated paradigm in politics. We can't continue to cast a blind eye to the existing intentional and unintentional barriers that prevent women from climbing the highest heights of Capitol Hill and government.

Wedding Bands Galore

Sixty-eight percent of "top-level" staffers are married. We're not sociologists, so we won't try to draw too many conclusions from this stat. Clearly, the marriage rate is significantly smaller at the entry-level positions, where we imagine most of you will find yourselves. We think we are safe to say, however, that the high marriage rate supports our general view that Capitol Hill, for all the late nights, bruising politics, and shredded nerves, is a place where one can settle down and build a family. We both met our spouses while working full-time on the Hill.

Diversity Doesn't Dominate, but It Is Desperately Needed

In addition, ninety-three percent of "top-level" Capitol Hill staff are white. We wish there was more diversity on Capitol Hill. When writing laws that impact all Americans, those who assist our lawmakers should reflect the diversity of America. A lack of diverse voices on the Hill and in politics in general was a driving force behind why Jaime first thought about writing this book. It's why Amos felt so inspired to have Jaime speak with the group of African American students on their first trip to Washington: Until listening to Jaime, some of them had never considered a job on Capitol Hill. This book aims to do more than simply encourage Americans of all backgrounds to explore a career in politics, it aims to *show* them how to climb the Hill.

Please don't let the rather homogenous nature of "top-level" staff dissuade you from going to Capitol Hill. We can guarantee that in other positions the range of people is far more eclectic and diverse than you might imagine. Nonetheless, these reports suggest that Capitol Hill and both major parties must address the lack of diversity among "top-level" staff.

Jaime often talks fondly about his experiences working for Democratic leadership on Capitol Hill. Yet, he also expresses his frustration that in some of the most meaningful and crucial policy discussions, he was the only or one of a few "top-level" staff of color in the room. As the first African American to serve as executive director of the House Democratic Caucus and floor director for the majority whip, Jaime's presence in these briefings, meetings, and strategy sessions meant that he was not only there to represent his interests or that of his boss, but he was obligated to shoulder the interests, concerns, and needs of all communities, particularly communities of color whose perspectives were not represented in the room. For a young staffer from a diverse community, the obligation to represent so many Americans could be a bit overwhelming, but until there are more diverse voices at the discussion tables in Congress and politics in general, it is an essential and necessary obligation.

America's greatest strength is its diversity. We are less than we can be when we do not utilize those diverse perspectives to craft legislation and make policy decisions that impact all Americans.

Our message to both political parties: Get your acts together and make sure that those leading and crafting policy also reflect the diversity of those impacted by that policy.

HOW QUICKLY CAN YOU CLIMB?

As for those other questions some of you might have for us, let's look at a couple more results from the *National Journal* survey.

- Almost half of top staffers have worked on the Hill fewer than ten years, and only eight staffers have thirty or more years of experience (in 2011).

- Of those surveyed, 59 percent have graduate degrees, with 35 percent being law degrees.

Both stats say to us something much different from what they might say to you. To the first question: Will it take me decades to reach the highest levels of Capitol Hill? The stat is ambiguous on this point, although it seems to say that the Hill is a transitory profession, with a bare few breaking into the top ranks. The answer, however, is an emphatic no. To the second question: Do you need an advanced degree to progress up Capitol Hill? The statistic seems to say yes, but the answer is also no.

Let's dissect the first question. Clearly, most staffers don't spend their entire careers on Capitol Hill. The survey tells us that the plurality of respondents (28 percent) had five to nine years' experience. That, in our experience, is about the length of most Capitol Hill "careers," although most fall more heavily on the longer side. There's a very simple explanation. The average tenure for a House representative, according to the Congressional Research Service, is 9.1 years. For senators, it's 10.2. In recent history, these averages have fluctuated very little and are almost always within a year or two of each other. Since most staffers don't outlast their member, there you are: a decade or less is the length of your typical Hill staffer career.

In that time—indeed, in half that time—one can rise to the highest positions. We did so. The Hill moves extremely fast, and those who can move with it will rise to the top. About the only credential one *needs* is a bachelor's degree to start the climb. The rest is up to you, and a little bit of Lady Luck. We've made the point, but it's worth reemphasizing: If you start in the House at an entry-level position (LA, LC, or the like), you will be given tasks and responsibilities far beyond what you'd get typically in another industry. Look at it this way: Congress is *set*, in that there are 535 members. It does not grow, except in very rare (in recent memory) circumstances—such as when another state is added to the union. While staff sizes have increased over the years, they're unlikely to increase in any significant way soon. Combine this with the ever-expanding responsibilities and problems confronting Congress (which are unlikely to decrease anytime soon), and you have a classic problem: worker shortage. This means for you, as it meant for us, that every staffer is important; every staffer has a job to do. There is more than enough work to go around.

Moreover, talent is rewarded. We can't say nepotism and plain old office politics don't exist, but both sooner or later succumb to the rigorous demands of the job. Those who can't perform eventually leave. Those who can, excel and advance. You will be surprised how quickly you can climb up the ladder in any office—assuming your member lasts beyond a single term.

Amos certainly was. If you remember, Amos was hired as a staff assistant for the House Energy and Commerce Committee. As an SA, Amos had pretty basic responsibilities. He answered the phones, helped set up the committee chamber for meetings, and delivered mail. Amos yearned for advancement, but committee staffs are tiny, which means unless the person above you moves on, where you are is where you stay. Even transitioning to a member's office was problematic because Amos got so little face time with the members themselves.

About the only good thing Amos could see was that he had about six hours of free time every day. He could have wasted those free hours; instead, he asked for more work. He had his eye on advancing to the committee press office, where he knew the skills he had learned at the PR firm would serve him well. On a regular basis, Amos asked the committee communications director if he could work in the press office. By this point, rejection didn't bother Amos. So rather than waste his day, Amos would search the Web to find media clips that the press office missed. He wasn't paid to do it, but he knew how to do it. Eventually the director began handing off small assignments to Amos. For example, some days he would peek his head in the office, look at Amos, and ask, "Can you type this into Word?" That led to more small assignments.

Then it happened. Amos had not been a staff assistant for even a year when the director came into the office he shared with the other assistants. The director pointed directly at Amos: "You're coming upstairs," he said. "Don't talk. Just answer the phone."

That's how Amos became a press assistant for the House Energy and Commerce Committee. The lesson of the story is that being persistent and helpful, and filling in the gaps can ultimately pay off. In politics, the cream definitely rises to the top, and the diligent tend to advance and are rewarded with promotion. Therefore, take advantage of opportunities and go over and beyond to perform.

DO YOU NEED AN ADVANCED DEGREE?

This leads us to the second stat on advanced degrees. We repeat: You don't need an advanced degree to work on Capitol Hill. But many staffers pursue an advanced degree *while on* Capitol Hill, because they're preparing for their post-Hill career. Given the nature of Hill work, it makes sense that many study law, although you will find MBAs and public policy, and a host of other master's degrees that relate to government work.

At the end of this book, we'll discuss a bit of post-Hill strategy. After all, neither one of us is still on the Hill, so it makes sense that we would have some suggestions in this regard. Pursuing an advanced degree is just such a strategy, but by no means the only one nor the easiest. Mind you, you would be studying whenever you aren't working, which isn't often. You will likely have to take out loans, which will further stress your already stressed staffer salary. It's not easy, is what we're saying. Jaime should know, since he got his law degree while he was a staffer.

As always, there are the caveats to the advanced degree question. For instance, if you find yourself on the policy track and come to enjoy one specific policy area—foreign policy, health care, or education, for example—there is a good argument that you should pursue an advanced degree in that area. If you gain a reputation as particularly adept at a certain issue, especially if you have an advanced degree to bolster your expertise, you will be sought after even if your member loses his or her seat or retires. In other words, being a policy expert, with a master's degree in that policy, can increase your long-term Hill employment prospects.

Policy experts also have another avenue open to them that is closed to most other staffers: committees. By and large, committees maintain the same "core" group of experts no matter who is the chair or which party is in power. Now, as a committee staffer you still must belong to one party and are subject to downsizing if your party loses committee control. But when you see that some staffers have been on the Hill twenty or thirty years or more, chances are they work for a committee. These folks are so expert in their field that even when their party is out of power, they survive—indeed, both parties rely on them to do the heavy lifting on legislative details.

A career in this field requires a deep passion for the policy itself—a passion that transcends politics. Despite all their hard work and long hours, often for very little gain (most bills never get past the committee phase to begin with), these folks never get the credit that is due to them. Of course, that's not why they do it. In any event, all we are saying is you'll know if this path is an option for you.

LESSON 8: "EXPERTS" HAVE AN ADVANTAGE

In politics, those hiring tend to look for those with a defined expertise or prior experience. Hence experts tend to have an advantage. This lesson is illustrated by Jaime's experiences.

When we left off, Jaime was an undergraduate at Yale. In his senior year he was accepted to Vanderbilt Law School in Nashville. But Jaime decided to defer law school for a year so that he could pursue another passion: teaching. After graduation, Jaime taught ninth-grade social studies for a year. He was preparing to attend Vanderbilt in the fall but was offered an amazing opportunity to serve as chief operations officer of College Summit, at the time the nation's largest nonprofit organization that helps low-income youth by connecting them to college and career.

In terms of Jaime's future Hill career, this job proved to be more than a footnote. It led him directly back to the Hill. College Summit was expanding its programs in South Carolina, and Jaime went to visit Senator Hollings, his old boss from his intern days. Hollings's chief of staff, Joey Lesesne, remembered Jaime from those days—and he remembered what an impression the young intern from Orangeburg had made on the entire office. After the meeting, Joey approached Jaime and offered him a job as legislative assistant in charge of education policy for the senator. The offer shocked Jaime, but it also proved all the lessons he had heard while an intern on the Hill: hard work pays off.

In the end, Jaime declined the offer. He had been at College Summit only a short time and was not ready to leave. However, the seed had been replanted: from then on, Jaime's mind was never far from Capitol Hill.

Two years later, Jaime's intern days paid off again. This time the offer came from Yebbie Watkins, chief of staff to Representative James Clyburn's office, with whom Jaime had worked closely years earlier. Clyburn had just been elected vice chair of the House Democratic

Caucus, which means the job offer came from a member of the party leadership. By this point, Jaime was in his second year at Georgetown Law, having given up his seat at Vanderbilt when he started with College Summit. Watkins's offer was as policy advisor to Clyburn, a significant position for someone as young as Jaime. He accepted.

In the last chapter, we joked that Jaime's return to the Hill was like being the top pick in the draft—at least compared to Amos. Whereas Amos had to claw his way onto the Hill, Jaime was actively recruited, not once but twice. That these offers came from the very offices where Jaime interned is only part of the story. The other part is that because of Jaime's experience at College Summit, not to mention his year of teaching, the Hill saw an education expert. Undoubtedly, his forthcoming Juris Doctor from Georgetown Law was also attractive in the Hill's eyes. But Jaime wasn't hired for his law knowledge; he was hired for his in-depth understanding of education policy and his connection to South Carolina.

This means little for the recent college graduate looking for a job on the Hill. Many may feel like political science experts after writing countless papers and sitting through hours of lectures for political science degrees. Regrettably, that doesn't give one expert status in politics. For recent graduates, academic knowledge must be coupled with actual experience. If it doesn't, you'll start at the bottom.

And it's why Jaime didn't start at the bottom. On his first day, Jaime was handed Clyburn's education docket—a massive compendium of education issues that dealt not only with South Carolina, but also with the entire nation. It was the very beginning of the new term, January 2003, and Clyburn was now in the leadership, which meant Jaime was staring at the education issues of the 204 other House Democrats of the 108th Congress. He barely had enough time to prepare for the Democratic Issues Conference, held at the end of January in Nemacolin, Pennsylvania, where he was expected to be the "face" of Clyburn's education policies, among several other issues.

Despite the tremendous pressure, Jaime was right where he wanted to be. Once a kid growing up in a poor neighborhood in South Carolina, Jaime was suddenly knocking elbows with Democratic powerhouses like representatives Nancy Pelosi, Steny Hoyer, John Lewis, and Bob Matsui. Even more remarkable, Jaime was seeing these pillars in the Democratic Party as they really were—real people, who were finally away from the bright, artificial glare of Washington. It was quite the introduction to Capitol Hill.

The honeymoon only lasted three days before Jaime was back in Washington, drowning in appropriations hell. It was the time of the congressional calendar when all the local earmark requests flooded the personal office. Maybe it wouldn't have been so bad if Jaime knew how appropriations worked. He didn't have a clue.

And he didn't have much time to learn. In desperation, he reached out to his office colleagues, the veterans who had been through an appropriations process before. Their advice was simple: See what's been done in the past and start there. Inspiring it was not, but extremely effective. Jaime got through it, even with a full course load from Georgetown Law. He learned a few things too, not least of which was how to get through your first appropriations process. The biggest lesson seems worth passing on to anyone in a similar situation: the Appropriations Committee is a creature of habit, in that it prefers funding programs that were funded in the past and is hesitant to fund new projects. That's about it.

Jaime also learned how powerful the leadership is within a caucus. He watched in awe as Minority Leader Nancy Pelosi handled and guided the caucus—no small feat when you're talking about more than two hundred individuals each trying to serve the needs of their constituents, not to mention prepare for reelection. The United States might be a democracy, but democracy doesn't always function democratically. It couldn't, not if there was any hope of getting stuff done. In Congress, hierarchy matters. Those at the top of the chain—the leadership—decide where to go; those underneath—everyone else—follow or are left behind. You don't want to be left behind.

During his first year in this, the lion's den of Congress, Jaime had to lean on his colleagues a lot to succeed. He also saw how Congress *really* operates, and it isn't how it looks on TV, or even how Jaime remembered from his intern days. But we'll get to all that later.

For now it's important to note that Jaime's first real job on the Hill, as a policy advisor to a member of the leadership staff, isn't exactly typical. If you're starting out, you shouldn't expect such a job. Which is far different from saying you shouldn't work for such a job. As someone with superb education credentials, Jaime could credibly claim that he probably knew more about education policy and the challenge in public schools than most. That certainly helps one just starting out. Nevertheless, Jaime needed a lot of help to get through that first year. He might have known a lot about education policy, but his colleagues knew far more than he about the day-to-day business of Congress.

So, while exhibiting "expert" credentials is a great way to break onto the Hill, never believe you know more than those who have been there longer than you.

LESSON 9: HOW DO YOU SWITCH CAREERS?

Jaime's story also offers some valuable insights into how one can switch careers and become a political staffer. As with most career switches, it's a lot harder than you might imagine. Fortunately, if you're patient—and if your ambition is realistic—you shouldn't have to start at the very bottom. Here are some useful pointers.

"Expert" Credentials

If you're an expert in a field relevant to the work of Congress and government, you have a good shot at moving into a midlevel position. We must warn you, however, that "typecasting" in politics, particularly on the Hill, is a problem. In other words, once you're known as an expert in a field, and only as an expert in a particular field, it's not terribly easy to move around. Even though Jaime was the "education guy," he quickly picked up an array of useful knowledge and skills that made him an invaluable team member. So, if you are an expert, live by the adage: No job is too small. It will help you tremendously later.

Policy, Nonprofit, Advocacy Work

If you already work in one of these fields, you'll have a nice advantage transitioning. You don't need to be an issues expert either. Communications, writing, strategy, and business development are all valued skills in politics, as long as you've gained these skills working in a relevant field. These types of shops also serve as good midpoints between your old career and politics. If you strike out landing a job, you should consider checking out job openings at these places where your acquired skill set would be valued. You're much more likely to get a job moving from the private sector to the nonprofit sector than directly into politics.

Writers Always Wanted

It's quite simple: If you can write—we mean, seriously write, with several samples to support your claim—you have a shot. In any political office, everyone knows the "writer," because he or she is one of the most important members on the team. Nearly everything you will be asked to do will involve writing of some sort, particularly at the midlevel positions. It's a skill that you could certainly learn, but offices much prefer to hire someone who already knows how to write. We cannot overemphasize this enough: good writers go to the head of the line.

Move to Washington (or to the Community in Which You Are Interested in Working)

You've heard us say this before. You can't undervalue the importance of living in Washington for getting a job on Capitol Hill or moving to the state capital if you are interested in a job in the state legislature. The people you meet, the events you can attend, the opportunities available—these are the things that simply cannot be had outside the location of the job. Especially if you have very little relevant experience going for you, you should consider packing and moving if you want to get that job.

First, Hire All the Lawyers

Of any single profession not directly related to government, lawyers are the most prevalent. Laugh if you want—and it is funny considering how many people with a Juris Doctor are running through the halls of Congress or serving in state legislatures—but being a lawyer opens numerous job opportunities otherwise shut off from everyone else. So, if you're in law school now and know you'd like to work in the government someday, don't fret so much about spending a few years at a firm or prosecutor's office. Get some experience first, then try your hand in politics.

Just Ask

As we've said, Capitol Hill and the political world in general are a pretty small and tight-knit community. Most folks were once where you are now, and they will be more than willing to offer help. We've stressed it before, but it bears repeating: just ask. Need a cheap place to live? Just ask. Wondering if it's okay to avoid the office happy hour? Just ask. Your more experienced and sometimes better-paid colleagues and contacts will perfectly understand your situation and accept your financially based limits, particularly as you engage in your search for the right position.

Chase the Coattails

We'll discuss campaign work in greater depth later. For now, if you're interested in changing careers, it's never a bad idea to sign on to a local campaign. Even if you have to start small, such as being a simple volunteer, you will meet the people who will be part of a congressional or state legislative office—assuming they win. This isn't quite as daunting a task as you might think. Congressional and state legislative campaigns happen every two years, and they're always short on two things: money and people. If you already have a job, offer your services after-hours. If the opportunity is there (and if you can afford to do so), by all means quit your current job and work full-time on the campaign. Many times, campaign staff get first dibs on office staff positions. The victorious member already knows who you are, how you work, and what your skills are. The member would much rather hire you than someone he or she doesn't know, but who might have more Hill experience. A note of caution, however—campaign staff are not always successful congressional or legislative staff. The mind-set and outlook are very different for these roles.

Changing careers is always a difficult task. But if you're willing to go that extra mile—find a job relevant to government work, move, or acquire an advanced degree—you have a good shot. Be daring; be bold; take a chance.

How They Climbed the Hill
ANANT RAUT'S STORY

It had been six months since I had applied for a position on the House Judiciary Committee, and I hadn't heard a peep. This was an odd experience for me. For my entire working life, after college and later, after law school, the process had been straightforward—you sent out your resume, you interviewed, and you chose. Rejection was a part of it too, and those form letters would arrive around the time you had inferred as much. But you always heard something. Silence was weird. Was I supposed to be doing something else? Needing answers, I called Jaime, whom I had known since we were undergrads at Yale. He was already something of a political superstar in the House of Representatives by this point.

Jaime was blunt: "Sending your resume isn't enough," he said. "You need to reach out to everyone you know on the Hill."

"You mean, just call them?" I asked.

"Yes."

And that's how I learned that even people with Ivy League pedigree still need to hustle if they want to land on the Hill. But self-promotion didn't come naturally to me. The son of Indian immigrants who came to America in the 1960s, I was raised on an ethos of hard work and humility. Keep your head down and let your work speak for you was the Asian American approach. This works off the Hill, particularly in the legal profession, where firms fight each other for the best talent. But on the Hill, I was just another lawyer looking for a job that hundreds of other qualified lawyers wanted just as badly.

The House Judiciary Committee wouldn't have been my first job in government. Fresh out of law school, I had worked at the Federal Trade Commission for a couple years before joining a private firm. My ambition was making partner, because—I don't know—that was the next shiny thing to be gotten on this track that I, like so many of my Harvard Law School classmates, ended up on by default. That all changed when I began pro bono representation of terror suspects in Guantanamo Bay. The experience opened my eyes to how much good can be accomplished with a law degree—and only a law degree. It also made me appreciate that the law is not some natural, fixed thing, but a set of rules that are only as good or as bad as Congress makes them. I became holistically aware of the law and the need for good lawyers in government.

So when a position opened up on the committee, I jumped at it . . . and waited. For months. After talking to Jaime, I started tapping my Yale and Harvard networks. For someone used to being self-reliant, I felt strange picking up the phone or sending an email to acquaintances and asking for help. But Jaime's advice was spot-on. Most everyone, it seems, got their start on the Hill because someone nudged their resume along. Credentials aren't enough on the Hill. You don't get jobs on the Hill because you know someone, but knowing someone on the Hill gets your resume in the pile that gets considered.

I was fortunate that I knew Jaime, and I was wise to follow his advice. I spent three amazing years as a counsel for the committee. Looking back, it was some of the most fun I've ever had at a job. Taking the Metro to work every morning, you scan the headlines like everyone around you, except you're picking out the issues you know you're going to have to address when you get to your desk. When law students and young lawyers ask me to compare working on the Hill versus working at a firm, I tell them that in the private sector, no one talks about how much things costs, but on the Hill, no one talks about how much they hate their job. People go to the Hill because they're passionate about trying to improve our country.

If you're looking to start on the Hill or transition to the Hill, my advice to you is simple, and it's the same advice Jaime gave me all those years ago: Reach out to everyone you know, even if you don't know them that well. More importantly, don't stop once you get there. The network you build on the Hill or elsewhere in politics will not just make you that much better at your job, it will also, and I say this from experience, last you a lifetime.

—**ANANT RAUT,** former special advisor to the Office
of Vice President Biden and President Obama's National
Economic Council

CHAPTER 5

REACHING THE SUMMIT

On the morning of Wednesday, November 8, 2006, congressional staffers woke up to a world turned upside down. During the midterm elections the previous night, Democrats had picked up thirty-one seats in the House of Representatives and captured the majority. In the Senate, the morning after saw a forty-seven to forty-nine split in favor of the Republicans, with two races still to be decided. But when incumbent senators George Allen of Virginia and Conrad Black of Montana conceded defeat over the next two days, Democrats won the Senate too. (Independent senators Bernie Sanders and Joe Lieberman would caucus with the Democrats.) The victory was so overwhelming that the Democrats did not lose a single incumbent or open seat in Congress.

A "wave election" like 2006 doesn't happen by surprise. Both the eventual winners and the losers prepare for it, even as the latter hold out hope for a miracle. But in this age of fine-tuned digital tools, miracles are rare. Amos recalls a dinner conversation he had with a veteran pollster a few days before the elections. When asked how bad a night it would be for the GOP, the pollster replied, "Unless North Korea attacks, Republicans are going to lose the majority." But what Amos heard was, "Start looking for a new job." You learn very quickly in politics that no job is safe and nothing is certain, particularly your job.

That's not because Amos's boss at the time, Representative Roy Blunt of Missouri, the majority whip, was in danger of losing reelection. Rather, members of the majority party in the House have twice the number of staff as the minority. It's an employment scheme that's baked into the House system. Which means that for the losing party, committees and leadership offices will lay off at least half of their staff when the new Congress takes over. Yes, losing control of the House of Representatives is a bloodbath for congressional staffers.

In theory, control of the House is contested every two years, when all 435 seats are up for election. Even for those who crave excitement and new experiences, looking for a job every two years would start to get frustrating. In practice, however, House turnover is rare. Since 1954, the House has changed hands just three times (1994, 2006, and 2010). Although the pace has quickened since 1994 for many reasons, none of which need occupy us here, incumbency is the greatest advantage in US politics.

Change of power in the Senate is more common. Since 1954, the Senate has changed hands seven times, most recently after the 2014 midterms when Republicans gained control. But even in the Senate, the majority party has an average tenure of eight years over the same period. Staff turnover in the Senate is also less dramatic since the larger staff sizes are less dependent on which party controls the chamber. But that doesn't mean losing control of the upper chamber is irrelevant for Senate staffers; as in the private sector, when your company hits hard times, heads roll.

On that Wednesday morning in 2006, we both awoke to a very different world. One of us, Jaime, was working as executive director for the chairman of the House Democratic Caucus, Representative James Clyburn. But Jaime knew that Clyburn would not remain caucus chairman for long; with the Democratic takeover, his boss was destined for larger things. Which meant that Jaime was destined for larger things. The other one, Amos, who by then was working for the Republican whip, was polishing his resume.

THE DIZZYING HEIGHTS OF LEADERSHIP

Until now, the lessons and nuggets of wisdom we've provided more or less mirror our ascent up Capitol Hill. At certain stages of your career on the Hill, some lessons are more important than others. We're going to depart from that structure for this chapter, which is the last one documenting our respective Hill careers. That's because while the lessons in this chapter come during our tenures in the leadership, they aren't exclusively "leadership lessons." They are universal lessons that, while not necessarily critical for your early days on Capitol Hill, will help you through every stage of your career.

Did we know these lessons before we reached the leadership? Perhaps in some cases, we did. But we certainly didn't appreciate their importance until we had reached the highest levels of Congress. Mountain climbers know that the higher they climb, the fewer mistakes they can afford to make. At those dizzying heights, with the lack of oxygen, the extreme cold, and the unpredictable weather, there is no room for error. A prick on a finger quickly escalates into gangrene. Frostbite on the nose means that, if you make it down, you'll need a good plastic surgeon. In short, the mistake that was forgivable working in Congress's backbenches becomes a fireable offense in the klieg lights of leadership work.

The sooner you learn these lessons, the better career you will have. The simple fact is that most staffers will never work in the leadership. This isn't a comment on the quality of the staffers; we mean that getting the opportunity to work for a member in the leadership is more luck than anything else. Sure, you can angle your career path in a leadership direction, but politics is an unpredictable mistress. Learn the famous axiom, The best laid plans of mice and men often go awry.

And sometimes those plans go exactly as planned, as Amos discovered. Earlier we discussed how Amos had been promoted to the press office of the House Energy and Commerce Committee. This was around 2004, and the GOP had held the House for almost ten years. It was also an election year, and Amos managed to split his time between the committee and assisting communications efforts for Louis Gohmert, a Republican member recently elected to Congress from Texas. The mixture of committee and communications work did wonders for boosting Amos's credentials. Remember, his only job on Capitol Hill to this point had been as a low-level communications staffer in a committee. It's not unimportant work by any means, but you rarely see your work in the news. A committee job is functional because a committee is functional. A committee doesn't look good or bad. It just does its job. If Amos was going to rise, he had to get creative in finding the right opportunities, even if it meant holding down two jobs.

More than anything, Amos wanted to work in a press shop for a member of the House leadership. So, in addition to his regular gigs, Amos studied the work of the press secretaries he admired. As a casual consumer of news, you might not look twice at a quote from a press secretary in an article. Or even a quote from a member. You probably didn't stop to think about how that quote was acquired, other than the reporter simply called and asked for one. But nothing goes in an article from a member's office that was not meticulously planned. (The unplanned quotes are the ones you don't want.) There's an art to it that we don't need to get into here, but that helps explain what Amos was studying.

If you want a taste of what this entails, do a quick news search of your House member. Click on any article and ask yourself these questions:

- What is the member's purpose in the article? Is he or she the subject? Or is the member there to explain, support, or deny an issue?

- Does the member come off looking good or bad? Either way, what gives you that impression? Is it how the reporter presents him or her? Or is it the quote that gives the impression?

- Who is quoted? Is it the member, the press secretary, the chief of staff? This is a critical point for any would-be press secretary. If the subject of the article is important to the member (in a good or bad way), you'll likely see the member quoted. If the member is only tangentially involved in the subject, you'll likely see a press secretary or chief of staff quoted.

- What other members are mentioned and/or quoted in the article?

- What type of publication is it? A national newspaper or magazine? A regional outlet? Is it a publication focused on Congress, like *Roll Call* or the *Hill*? Or is it a partisan outlet, like *National Review* on the Right or the *New Republic* on the Left?

In this way, you can study how a member's press shop operates. You can see what issues the member likes to be in front of and which ones he or she doesn't. You can see which outlets the member values and which ones are left to subordinates. Then you can start to make some subjective insights. For instance, your studying told you that this member wants to be out front on foreign policy issues. So why wasn't he or she quoted in this major *New York Times* story on foreign policy? A reporter wants to quote the most insightful and relevant (and provocative) members for any article. The *New York Times* "miss" reflects badly not on the member, but on his or her press shop: The staffers aren't doing their job thoroughly enough. Likewise, why did the *Washington Post* run an entire article on this backbencher's tax policy views? If you think that the press shop was waiting around for a call from a reporter, you need to study more. That "hit" was the result of weeks-long—sometimes months-long—efforts, likely initiated by the member's staff, to help raise his or her profile on a valued issue. When the article runs—assuming it reflects well on the member—the champagne is already on ice because the victory party was planned long before.

This is what constituted Amos's studying. This is how he learned his craft or, rather, the game. The game consists of a daily race between member press shops to procure the best possible coverage for their boss. Sometimes that means no coverage at all. And sometimes that means your boss is sitting at the table of *Meet the Press*. But in the end, it's a game—a game whose rules, tactics, and strategies are obscure to the general public, but which must be mastered by the competent press secretary on Capitol Hill. Amos's work on the committee and for Gohmert introduced him to the general rules, but it wasn't until he started to study the press secretaries he admired that he really learned how to play.

But, remember, politics is unpredictable. And how we consume and share news is forever evolving. That's the attitude that helped Amos evolve his career when blogging started to gain popularity and power in the media universe.

Prior to the 2004 presidential election, blogs were mostly ignored by the media and much of Washington. The few that existed were written by relative no-name "amateurs," many of whom had day jobs outside politics or journalism. But during the election, blogs made their presence—and power—known following a *60 Minutes II* story on President George W. Bush's tenure in the Texas Air National Guard. You might have heard about it. The story centered on memos supposedly written by Bush's superiors criticizing the young pilot of shirking his guard duties. The story aired September 2004, just two months before Election Day, and promised to deliver a blow to Bush's reelection chances. Yet within hours of the story's airing, the derided blogs had jumped on it—and tore it to shreds. Employing the then new power of digital technology, the blogs showed that the memos were forgeries. It was a nice feather in the cap of a rising media power.

But by the winter of 2005, blogs had shown to be more than mere fact-checkers. The partisan ones had acquired a large readership, and they were able to use that readership to effect change in Washington. During the Blunt-Boehner battle for majority leader in September

2005, the conservative blogs lined up behind Boehner and used their power to push him to victory. Blunt would remain majority whip. Suddenly the whole makeup of the Republican leadership had changed, and the blogs could legitimately claim it was their doing. It was a wake-up call for every member in Congress. There was a new player in town, and one crossed Blunt at his peril.

Watching from afar, Amos saw what happened. More importantly, he saw the power of the blogs. When a chance encounter with the husband of a Blunt staffer revealed to Amos an open position in the whip's press office, he jumped on it. Amos remembers vividly the day of the interview, walking from his office on the fifth floor of the Cannon House Office Building—a floor so unloved the elevator stopped at the fourth floor—through the offices to the Capitol and up to Statuary Hall, where Blunt had his office. Amos was standing near the summit of Capitol Hill, and he desperately wanted to plant his flag.

It was at this moment that Amos's preparation, his studying, paid off. He nailed the interview and got the job later that week. One of his first assignments in the press office of the House majority whip? Fix the blog situation.

LESSON 10: POLITICS ISN'T A GAME; IT'S JUST PLAYED LIKE ONE

How did Amos, a staffer on a committee, land a job in the leadership? Sure, luck had something to do with it. But in Amos's determination to work in a leadership office, he learned how to play the press game. He wasn't a master of it by any means (as we'll see in a moment), but he could talk intelligently about matters with which he had had no direct experience. He had learned enough in his few, brief years on the Hill to know that those who play the game well get results.

Washington politics is often derided as a game. There's certainly plenty of buffoonery going on to make it seem like one. But those who have spent any significant time in Washington and on Capitol Hill know that it's not. They see that those politicians and those staffers who treat their work like a game aren't around for long. Politics is a serious business and it demands serious people. The purpose of getting the right "hit" in the news isn't to gratify your ego-driven boss (well . . . not usually); it's to get his or her message across to the right people, at the right time. While a casual consumer of news might not care who is quoted where, that's how things happen on Capitol Hill. The right person reads the right story at the right time, and there's your boss, front and center. A call is made. A meeting is scheduled. An idea is formed. A bill is drafted. A vote is called. A law is passed. This process can take years and often does. But the seeds of success or failure are sprinkled on the hundreds of articles published every day—or hour, in our digital media world.

But to see that kind of success requires strategy—and strategy is at the heart of every game invented. You need to know the right time to put your boss forward and when to hold back. You need to know the right words to use and which ones to avoid. You need to know what message will reach the right ears and which outlets will reach the right eyes. This doesn't happen randomly. Luck plays a part, but in politics, one must create luck. No team has reached the Super Bowl without its fair share of lucky breaks—when the ball bounces your way. But no bad team has ever reached the Super Bowl. You get to the top by playing the game well. And that takes a serious mind.

While Amos had put in the hard work before he achieved his dream of working in a leadership press office, he still had much to learn about how to play the game. One morning early in the week, Amos fielded a call from a producer for *Meet the Press*. The producer asked if Representative Blunt would be available for that Sunday's show. Amos was still new at the job, and the thought of booking a "hit" on *Meet the Press* for his boss was tantalizing. Without asking anyone else, he told the producer, yes, Mr. Blunt was available. The producer would call back later.

Excited, Amos raced to tell the news to his superior. Instead of giving him a hearty slap on the back for a job well done, she asked, "Why did you do that?" She was upset that Amos had accepted the interview so quickly, because she knew that they wouldn't get it. It was then that Amos learned an important lesson about media in the big leagues: It's a game. The press wants to book the most in-demand politicians they can. They want to beat their competition with the bigger "get," the bigger name. They want to brag that they were able to land the majority whip when *Face the Nation* couldn't. But how in demand is someone who isn't busy on a Sunday morning? When Amos said yes immediately, the first thought in the producer's mind was probably: "I guess *Face the Nation* or *This Week* hadn't called." But if you're someone worth having, they all call you. As it happened, Amos's superior was right: the majority whip wasn't on *Meet the Press* that Sunday.

The game isn't confined to media. For every position on Capitol Hill, in every office, there's a way to get the best results for your member. You can say there's a nuance to the politics of politics. You won't understand it immediately; it will likely take years to fully master the rules of your particular game. But it's never too soon to start learning. Once you've decided what you want to do on Capitol Hill, communications or policy, you must start learning how to get results. Even if the big boys and girls won't let you play yet, you can always watch, ask questions, and beg to be put in.

LESSON II: ALWAYS PROTECT YOUR BOSS

Let's return now to Jaime's story. Jaime had just accepted a position on Representative Clyburn's staff as a policy advisor specializing in education. It was 2003, and Clyburn was the vice chair of the Democratic Caucus, which meant that Jaime was working in the leadership. When the 2006 midterms rolled around, Jaime was a veteran of Capitol Hill and part of Clyburn's inner brain trust. This gave him invaluable insight into the workings of Capitol Hill and allowed him to see opportunities and threats that could impact his boss's future in Congress and leadership.

One notable instance occurred after the Democrats' sweep of Congress. The Democrats were busy forming the leadership team for their new House majority, and Jaime was watching the leadership story unfold from the inside. In theory, both parties follow a hierarchical approach to leadership positions. For instance, the minority leader becomes the Speaker, the whip becomes majority leader, the caucus chair becomes majority whip and so on. The position of Speaker was settled and uncontested. On November 16, 2006, a week after the midterms, Nancy Pelosi, then minority leader, was unanimously chosen by the House Democratic Caucus as the new Speaker of the House—the first woman Speaker in US history. But that's where the era of good feelings ended.

Months earlier, Representative Jack Murtha of Pennsylvania decided to oppose the minority whip, Steny Hoyer of Maryland, for the position right below Speaker: majority leader. Most members of the Caucus thought that the other races would remain uncontested. As chair of the House Democratic Caucus, Representative Clyburn was the third- ranking Democrat in House leadership and the highest-ranking African American in Congress. Clyburn, like Pelosi and Hoyer, had made it known early that he wanted to maintain his slot as the third-ranking Democrat and worked tirelessly to elect Democrats to gain the majority. Representative Rahm Emanuel from Illinois was the chair of the Democratic Congressional Committee and the fifth-ranking Democrat. He helped to oversee the successful effort to win the majority and decided that he wanted to run for the whip position. That meant a contest against Representative Clyburn, Jaime's boss.

Given that there was now a contested race, representatives Clyburn, G. K. Butterfield of North Carolina, Clyburn's chief of staff Yebbie Watkins, and Jaime met to settle on strategy and to mobilize internal and external support for Clyburn. They knew that Clyburn had to secure votes of key members across a diverse caucus and the Congressional Black Caucus (CBC) could help them do that. Clyburn immediately began his calls to secure support from key members. Representative Butterfield, Yebbie, and Jaime developed the case for why Clyburn should be elected whip, and they educated CBC members and other Clyburn allies and supporters about the race. Through the press, Rahm and his allies tried to make the contest about temperament for the job, but many saw the race as an attack on the well-established congressional seniority system, a system that would help create a historic number (five) of African American committee chairs in the new majority. Butterfield, Yebbie, and Jaime knew that Clyburn's greatest assets were his kinship with his colleagues in the CBC (who represented one-third of the vote needed to win) and the respect Clyburn garnered from colleagues across the caucus. Ultimately, it was the CBC's unwavering support and vociferous advocacy coupled with Nancy Pelosi's focus on keeping harmony with her slim majority that resolved the short-lived contest. In the end, Clyburn became majority whip and Rahm assumed the fourth-ranking position of caucus chair.

You don't have to be in leadership to witness this type of hardball politics. It happens at all levels of Congress. But when you are in leadership, the stakes are higher. In these situations, how does one proceed? It comes down to a simple lesson: Always assess the opportunities and threats of a situation, and use the strongest and most-available assets to assist and protect your boss. That's it. When in doubt on the way forward, protect your boss.

Yes, there are exceptions to this lesson, which we'll discuss in a later chapter. **We are not saying, however, that you should protect your boss or interfere when dealing with anything criminal, illegal, or against congressional ethics rules.** Common sense goes a long way on the Hill, as does a good moral compass. **Nor should you accept any abuse, physical, sexual, or verbal, that makes you uncomfortable or causes you pain.** Your member is your boss, not your monarch. But if the grand sum of our experiences on Capitol Hill can be boiled into one, overriding rule, this is it. The hard reality is that on Capitol Hill your career is built around your boss. If he or she loses an election, you lose an election. If he or she doesn't rise in the party hierarchy, you don't rise in the party hierarchy. If he or she falls, you fall as well. Protecting your boss isn't just a way to look good; it's the only way one moves up the Hill. In other words, when you protect your boss, you protect yourself.

During the leadership elections in the winter of 2006, Jaime saw the threats to his boss's future in leadership, assessed the best path to negate that threat, and ultimately protected his boss. And his boss, Representative Clyburn, became majority whip. As a result, Jaime worked for the third-highest-ranking member in the House and ran the whip operation for House Democrats as floor director. That's where he would end his Hill career, but we'll get to that later.

LESSON 12: IT'S NEVER AS BAD (OR GOOD) AS IT LOOKS

Things also ended well for Amos in the aftermath of the 2006 midterms. Even as he saw dozens of his colleagues lose their jobs, Amos kept his. But in Congress the sting of defeat lingers long after the ballots are counted. The Senate operates in a way where the minority still holds a lot of power; they can block legislation, for instance. But in the House, matters are more mathematical. You don't have the numbers; you don't have the power. Amos and the other Republican staffers learned to get along even though the power their party had held since 1994 had disappeared. He remembers quite clearly in the days after the election, as he and his fellow Republican staffers were busy scheduling job interviews, Pelosi's staff began evaluating the leadership conference rooms. It was certainly the worst of times for Republicans.

Here's the final lesson we'll impart in this section of the book. Four years later, after both of us had left Congress, the Republicans recaptured the House. Four years after that, in the midterms of 2014, they recaptured the Senate. At the time of the Democratic takeover in 2006, dozens of stories predicted a new reign of Democratic dominance in Congress. The so-called Republican Revolution of 1994 turned out to be nothing more than an anomaly, a blip in the natural order of things. So much for all that.

Not just in electoral politics but also in the legislative arena, things are never as bad, or as good, as they seem. Defeat stings. And victory tastes very sweet. As a staffer, you will experience both. We hope you have more victories than defeats, but whatever happens, remember this: Take it all in stride. The cycle of Capitol Hill is such that election battles are quickly followed by legislative battles, which are followed by election battles. At each turn of the wheel, there are a multitude of opportunities for victory and defeat. However the chips fall, take it in stride. After a particularly fulfilling victory, you will be tempted to rub it in the opposition's face. Don't. Get on with your job.

And when you're down, bruised from a fierce defeat, you might be tempted to turn cynical. You might tell yourself that all your hard work was for nothing. Don't. Pick yourself up and remember that things are never as bad as they seem.

Politics, after all, is an unpredictable sport.

How They Climbed the Hill
AARON LATHAM'S STORY

It was somewhere in the middle of my third interview for a job as communications director on the Hill that I thought, "Man, this is really tough." The third interview was the first one where I talked to the congressman himself, Representative Patrick McHenry from North Carolina's Tenth District. The first two had been more like screening interviews. Did I know the issues? Did I know what mattered to the member's constituents? Could I speak coherently without drooling all over myself? Apparently, the answers were yes, because here I was, finally sitting down with the boss.

But let me back up. Amos and I have known each other almost our whole lives. His mother was my sixth-grade math teacher, if that gives you any clue on the longevity of our friendship. When I first came to Washington, where Amos was already firmly ensconced, I didn't know a soul—except for him, but I hadn't talked to Amos in years. No matter. I emailed him, just to let him know I was moving to DC, only to have him say that he would pick me up at the airport.

I was in town for my first Hill internship. The experience only confirmed my ambition to live and work in Washington, preferably on the Hill, but I was flexible. After the internship, I earned a master's, did some teaching, and worked at a PR firm. It was around this point in my career, when I was still in my midtwenties, that I attacked the Hill full force looking for a press secretary or communications director job. And that's what brought me to the attention of McHenry's office. The congressman was the youngest member on the Hill and from a region of the country that somewhat mirrored my home, Alabama.

My first interview was with the chief of staff and legislative director. As I mentioned, the questions were general, but also pointed. They wanted to know if I had done my homework. (I had.) I could speak intelligently on the issues that mattered to the congressman and his district. The second interview was more of the same. The third was with McHenry, who grilled me on the issues, testing me on how well I knew his positions. We covered them all: immigration, Second Amendment, budget, taxes, and so on. I like to think I passed with flying colors. Then came the curveball.

"Of my positions, which ones do you disagree with?" he asked me. I had prepared for every question, except this one. Saying I agreed with him on every issue was no good. Too transparent. Too obsequious. So I chose honesty, telling him I disagreed with him somewhat on the Second Amendment, specifically as it related to allowing the purchase of assault rifles. He heard my objections, defended his position, and took me over to a computer terminal.

"You have ten minutes to write a one-minute speech defending my full support of the Second Amendment," he told me, adding, "specifically, on allowing the purchase of assault rifles." Then he walked out of the room.

"Damn, this guy is good," I thought.

Ten minutes later, the chief of staff came in, looked at my work, and thanked me. Did I pass? Well, I got a call asking me to come in for the fourth interview. By the way, there would be seven interviews in total. Thankfully, four through six were much less formal. I got the sense that they believed I had the skills for the job but wanted to know if I was a good fit for the office. I spent the sixth interview at a restaurant with the chief of staff and political advisor, talking about sports. The interview ended when the political advisor suddenly said to me, "Aaron, spell *maintenance*."

It was only when I left—having spelled it correctly—that I saw that over my shoulder, where the advisor had been looking, was a sign for the maintenance room. Yeah, they were good.

The final interview was with the congressman again—only this time I was asked to meet him in North Carolina. And I had to get there myself, which meant scrounging up a few hundred bucks for a plane ticket. I met the chief of staff at the airport, and we drove to a restaurant. An empty restaurant, with only a couple of servers. The chief left and the congressman entered.

It wasn't an interview; it was a job offer. "Aaron," he said, "we wanted someone who was willing to make a personal sacrifice to join our team. You did that. The job is yours."

I flew home and gave my two weeks' notice.

—**AARON LATHAM,** public policy manager, Alabama
Power Company

CHAPTER 6

EXPLORING ALTERNATE ROUTES

The number of congressional staffers hovers around fifteen thousand, not including employees in the various research arms of Congress and the security branches. That might seem like a lot, but a point we've tried to emphasize throughout this book is that each one of those fifteen thousand jobs is highly prized, and only a fraction are open at any given time. Our entire purpose in writing this book is to give you a significant boost in landing one of those open positions and then making the most of it when you do.

Nevertheless, the odds are never in your favor as an untried, untested applicant on Capitol Hill. One obvious solution is to be both tried and tested when you apply. How so? For starters, there are fifty state legislatures and thousands of city and municipal governments. While still very competitive, staff positions at the state and local level are great ways to earn some political experience and make connections before you try for Capitol Hill. You also may decide that you want to stay local, or perhaps you never had any desire to work in Washington, DC.

This chapter is to help you expand your horizons when thinking about a job in politics. We don't want to limit our discussion to Congress or Washington, DC. Some of the best work that one can do as a staffer takes place at the local level. If your goal is to make a difference, we encourage you to look at what's happening in your own state and city or town. Likewise, each of the two major political parties has its national organization as well as campaign committees that work closely with

Capitol Hill. Particularly during election season, these organizations are often starved for labor—that is, someone hungry for a job in politics. Someone just like you. State legislatures and political committees also provide great alternatives when looking for summer internships.

As we said earlier, we have used "the Hill" as a catchall that includes political work at both state and local level. That said, there remain differences between national political work and state and local work—differences that we will try to explain in this chapter. The problem is that there are fifty state legislatures and thousands of city and municipal governments. We can't list all of their unique features, even if we knew them, other than to say that each is unique in its own way, just as Capitol Hill is unique. We don't want to give the impression that these other Off the Hill options are interchangeable with the Hill. There is a huge difference between working at the state or local level or for a national party committee.

Our hope is that after reading this chapter, some of you will say, "You know, I think I'd rather try to make a difference locally in my home state." Or, "It sounds like a campaign committee is more what I'm looking for." If so, we will have done our job.

THE MINOR LEAGUES?

Let's start at the state and local level. Our first task is to eliminate any notion you might have that these jobs are lesser than Capitol Hill work. It's a shame that so much of our political focus is on Washington, Congress, and the White House. It makes sense, but the attention also distorts the public's view on how our federal system operates. Young people might think that the only worthwhile political work happens on Capitol Hill. This is wrong. Your city council and state legislature have a far greater impact on your life than Washington, DC, does.

Now *impact* isn't easy to define. Neither state nor city governments have much to say about whether the country goes to war or setting national economic policy. Clearly those issues have a large impact on your life. But on the day-to-day items, the issues that directly affect *you,* there's no comparison. Are your roads paved or schools funded? Does your state attract more residents than move away? What's the business climate like in your state or city? These are all state and local issues.

National politics is exciting and seemingly consequential, but a lot of it is political theater. State and local governments certainly have their own drama—peruse the metro section of your newspaper—but they are also under greater pressure to *get things done*. State and local governments don't have the luxury of delaying school funding or letting an infrastructure-spending bill lapse until next year. City governments can't wait for Washington to figure out what to do about pressing local issues, such as crime. State governments need to incentivize both businesses and residents to move in instead of out.

What we're saying is that things *happen* at the local level at a rate that they don't on Capitol Hill. More importantly, the issues on the table and the bills that pass have an immediate and direct impact on your neighbors, your family, and you. The link between your work and what happens is more solid than if you worked in Congress. The stage might seem smaller, but that's only if you measure it by media coverage. If you measure it by the impact *you* could have, it's much larger than Capitol Hill.

Politics of the sort that occupies our cable news does happen at the state and local level. But it's localized. Meaning if you only follow national politics, you would have little reason to know much about what's going on in your state. We all do this, because, frankly, national politics is fun to follow; state politics, outside of elections, is work-a-day stuff. But that also tells you all you need to know about the differences between the state legislature and Capitol Hill. The work one does at the state and local level is often relegated to the back pages. The drama is rarely on the level that captures a ton of eyeballs. But that doesn't make it any less important. Quite the contrary, it's vital to the functioning of the country.

Regardless, state and local work isn't the minor leagues. This work isn't a "step down," after you failed to land a job on the Hill. If you treat it as such, you will fail. State and local positions can be used to land a career in Washington, so don't act like you have better things to do than whatever your state legislator has you doing. When you get a job at the state capitol or on the city council, you've entered the big leagues. Play like a champion.

WHY GO LOCAL?

Washington, DC, may get much of the political spotlight, but most of the work of governing takes place on a local level and in state capitols. There are some good and practical reasons one might prefer to build a career at the state and local level than in Washington. Let's look at a few.

1. Big Fish, Small Pond

With fifteen thousand staffers, Capitol Hill might feel like a big place. But spend a few months there, and you'll quickly realize how small the community is. Now consider that more than thirty-one thousand staffers work in all the state legislatures combined. That means there are around six hundred staffers per legislature. Of course, dividing by fifty isn't proper, because some state legislatures are much bigger than others. Texas has the most legislative staffers, at twenty-three hundred, and Vermont the smallest state capitol staff, at ninety-two. Despite their sizes, small legislative communities make huge decisions. As we said above, state governments need to get things done to a degree that makes Capitol Hill feel like it moves at a snail's pace. Now also consider that most state legislatures are part-time or have extended recesses throughout the year, cramming all the real work into a short legislative session, and you can begin to imagine the scope of the work as a staffer.

As a staffer at the state level, you will be expected to handle a diverse set of responsibilities and tasks. Although this varies from statehouse to statehouse, you won't be subjected to the same restrictions and strict hierarchy that reign on the Hill. You will meet the most powerful legislators as well as civic and business leaders of your state. Given the small office sizes, you will wear many hats. Divisions of labor aren't as specific as they are in Washington, which means you will learn a little bit of everything, from communications to policy to plain ol' politicking.

The benefit is that you will become a known and important person at the capitol in a much shorter time than in DC. You will learn the political and legislative game much quicker, and be able to influence events much sooner. It's not Washington, but then most presidents don't come from Congress. They come from the states, from the governor's mansions. You will know your governor, perhaps even on a first-name basis. You will know your legislators, who will be much more your equal. And you will know your constituents, their concerns, their fears, their dreams—and they will know you.

2. A Network of Possibilities

We repeat: Often presidents come from governor's mansions. Governors come from state capitols. You work in the state capitol. See the possibilities? We will discuss in greater length the importance of your network in a later chapter. But if you consider all we said about the intimacy of a state capitol, the closeness you will have with the powers that move your state, you should begin to understand that working at the state level puts you in a prime position to meet all the right people.

It won't feel like it right away. You will be working in a very small office. But statehouses are deceptive like that—they aren't grandiose, and they don't get the prime-time coverage—and yet they are where the future leaders of the nation often start. On the legislative floor, in the courthouses, at the governor's mansion—as a staffer, you will be at every one.

As on Capitol Hill, you will find that your fortunes are attached to those of your legislator. But at the state and local level, that attachment is even more intimate. The divisions between Hill staff and district staff, such as on the Hill, don't exist at the state level. The political, policy, and communication brain trust that a legislator has is usually with him or her all the time, in the office, on the trail, and up the political ladder. Also keep in mind that in legislatures, particularly those that are part-time, legislative staff are likely shared by multiple members. Hence, it is likely that you will have more than one boss, a big contrast from working on Capitol Hill. As a function of small legislative staffs, an additional contrast to staff life on Capitol Hill is that sometimes you may even find yourself working for legislators of rival parties. Nonetheless, if you find yourself working for legislators who rise high, it is likely that you will too.

The sheer quantity and quality of connections you can make at the state level will allow you to take your career in any number of exciting directions. The difference between your network at the state level versus in Washington is one of diversity. Most people who work in politics in DC only work in politics. This fact makes the political community feel connected and close-knit, but also somewhat insular. Conversely, many people who work in politics at the state level often have other jobs—even the legislator for whom you work. Politics is much more a second job than a full-time pursuit and for very clear reasons: the legislative sessions are short, and people need to make a living. What this means for your network is that you will meet people from all walks of life, in many different professions.

That doesn't make a state staffer's network better than a Hill staffer's. "Better" is entirely relative in this case. But your network will be the envy of your nonstaffer friends. You will be able to leverage your network in ways that could take your career on many successful paths. Even to the White House.

3. Home Sweet Home

Nothing compares to the feeling of helping the people in a state or city you call home. In Washington, the connection to the public, your constituents, is never far from your mind, but it is far from you. Washington DC is also where the big media outlets, lobbying firms, consulting agencies, and communication companies have their head-quarters. With such a heavy concentration of politically connected organizations, it's no wonder that, as a group, Washingtonians sometimes suffer from a severe case of DC-itis. In other words, they come to believe that everything important in the world happens in Washington, and everything else, outside.

When you work at the state or local level, you don't have to worry about DC-itis. The connection you have with those you are fighting for is much closer, both figuratively and literally. It's easier to stay focused if you see the product of your work in the land and people around you. It's also harder to become cynical when you work on behalf of your neighbors, friends, and family. Your desire to "make a difference" means so much more when the difference you are making is right in front of your eyes.

We mention this because politics is a personal pursuit. You can work for a company and not particularly care about the product or service that company sells. But it's next to impossible to work in politics and not care about what you're doing or why you're doing it. It doesn't work. Some of you might think that you would never lose your passion working on Capitol Hill, but we see it happen all the time. We can only speculate, but many who do probably stop seeing (or never saw) the actual benefits of their work. They lose their passion because so much of it is wrapped up in ideology and gridiron politics. While those can be rewarding passions, they also can feel like a dog chasing its tail. Progress is hard and fleeting.

Which is why working for your home can be such a rewarding experience. It's why Jaime went to work as the chairman of the South Carolina Democratic Party. There's a reason so many people "go home" after college or after a few years away in the workforce. The ties to home have as much to do with people's career choices as a paycheck. There's absolutely no shame in it; in fact, being home may contribute significantly to your overall happiness.

So, the question is, Do you pack up and move to a strange, expensive town that runs day and night on politics? Or do you stay home and help make a difference for your friends and family? Only you can determine the right choice. But we want to make you aware that choosing the latter is a worthwhile, noble, and ultimately rewarding one.

THE POLITICAL COMMITTEES

The other Off the Hill options we'll discuss in this chapter are the national party committees and their respective Hill committees. We assume that many of you are aware of what these organizations do, at least broadly, so we won't get into too much detail. Yet there are likely some misconceptions and confusion surrounding them and their official responsibilities, so a quick refresher is in order. Let's start with the national party committees.

Democratic National Committee (DNC) and Republican National Committee (RNC)

People who otherwise might be unfamiliar with the main duties of the RNC and the DNC likely know that they have something to do with the presidential nominations. That notion would be right. Each national party committee oversees its respective party's presidential nomination process, presidential primary debates, presidential convention, and delegate selection process. It also oversees the activities of party committees in each state and the national coordination of outreach to various constituencies. Jaime ran for chair of the Democratic National Committee and currently serves as the associate chair and counselor for the Democratic National Committee.

The nominating conventions held by each major party every four years are big, ostentatious affairs that are widely covered by the media. Today, the conventions are little more than celebrations for the nominee's general election campaign. The way the modern primary system works means that the nominee is already known going into the convention, where the state delegates merely certify the choice of the voters. It wasn't always like this. Nomination conventions used to be bare-knuckle, backroom politics at its finest—or worst, depending on your perspective. Several presidential candidates would go into the multiday convention not knowing who would come out as the nominee. Multiple ballots of the delegates would eventually whittle down the choices until one person was left standing.

Things are different today. And while the excitement and tension have given way to four-day crowning ceremonies, the conventions are still great political theater. They introduce the presidential candidate to the public, which very likely has paid little attention to the primaries until this point. When the conventions are over, the general election officially has begun.

But conventions are just one part of the what the RNC and DNC do. In brief, each organization acts as national headquarters for all official party business, from campaigns to platforms to fund-raising—lots and lots of fund-raising. The national committees also coordinate with their state counterparts, such as the South Carolina Democratic Party, where Jaime was chair, to elect their party candidates in statewide and local elections. Historically, the bulk of the national committees' work is on the national level.

Jobs at the national committees in part mimic aspects of political campaigns. However, there are also positions oriented toward the operating functions of the committee. Traditionally, each committee would contain the following core departments.

- Executive—office of the chair and CEO/executive director

- Political

- Finance

- Research

- Communications

- Digital and data

- Party administration and affairs

- Secretary's office

In addition to these departments, each national committee commits staff and resources to reach out and manage relationships among its chief constituency groups. For example, the Democratic National Committee has fourteen constituency caucuses and councils that include African American, Native American, Hispanic, Asian Pacific Islander, disabilities, veteran, rural, and faith groups.

The DNC and RNC also have year-long intern and fellowship programs. Interns for these programs are assigned to various departments in each committee to get a better understanding of the day-to-day operation of the national committees.

Also, don't forget there are more than fifty state party committees. Jaime ran one of these smaller committees. In many ways, they operate like start-ups. State Party Committees have more freedom to experiment and explore new campaign techniques. As a state party chair, Jaime created new initiatives like Democrats Care, a community service based program. These smaller organizations are constantly looking for talent to fill full-time positions and internships.

Hill and Governors Committees

Each of the major political parties has an election committee that focuses on House, Senate, and gubernatorial races. These committees are the Democratic Congressional Campaign Committee (DCCC), Democratic Senate Campaign Committee (DSCC), Democratic Governors Association (DGA), National Republican Congressional Committee (NRCC), National Republican Senatorial Committee (NRSC), and Republican Governors Association (RGA). Smaller election committees or associations focus on legislative, attorneys general, secretaries of state, mayoral, and municipal elections.

It's important to note that these committees are more closely connected to the party leadership in Congress or the nation's governors as opposed to being arms of the national committees. One big example of that is that each of the six committees has a sitting member of Congress or governor as its head, whereas the national committees don't.

The House and Senate governors committees have dual missions: protect incumbents by getting their people reelected and increase their membership by defeating candidates from the other party. They do this through fund-raising and coordination of efforts with national, state, and local campaigns and parties. Fund-raising is probably the most important function of these committees. These committees, along with the national party committees, are the source of the hundreds of political fund-raising appeals you receive every year. Despite raising hundreds of millions, the committees can't support every race; they need to be strategic about which races they throw their weight behind. Often, they help state parties recruit the right kind of candidate—the one most likely to win given the district's demographics. But the end is the same. They exist to help their parties win and increase their seats in each congressional chamber and the governor's mansions.

If you want to focus on the campaign and hard-nosed politics above policy and constituent services, you'll probably enjoy working on a Hill or governors committee. You won't be parsing the intricacies of an appropriations bill; you'll be working on political outreach or upgrading the committee's digital outreach efforts. You won't be fielding angry constituent phone calls; you'll be fielding angry candidate phone calls. You won't be trying to find compromise with the other side; you'll be doing opposition research to crush a candidate on the other side.

Sounds like fun, right? It certainly can be if that's what you want to do. But what do you think the mood was like in the offices of the National Republican Congressional Committee on November 8, 2006, the day after the Democrats recaptured control of the House of Representatives?

Or how about at the Democratic Congressional Campaign Committee the morning of November 3, 2010, when the Republicans took it back? After each huge defeat, heads roll at the Hill committees. Not everyone gets the boot, and if you're low enough you might survive, but the amount of blame a Hill committee receives after a crushing blow can be devastating. In the one job you or your colleagues are paid to do, everyone failed. These committees are fast paced and exciting, but sometimes staff tenures can be short—lasting one or two cycles, or changing when a new chair takes the helm. It's something to keep in mind if you're weighing the Hill committees against Capitol Hill.

Also keep in mind that you will have very strong ties to Capitol Hill, both members and staff. Many of our friends and colleagues moved back and forth between the Hill committees and Capitol Hill, because the link between the two is so close. This revolving-door nature of the Hill committees shows that, while the work is different from that on Capitol Hill, it is also complementary. Working on the Hill will show you how to get legislative results; working on a Hill committee will show you how to get electoral results. You can't disassociate politics from legislating, and the best staffers (of either organization) know both.

The Hill committees can be a doorway to Congress. But we should add a caveat. They need "party people," those who are loyal members of the party from the moment they apply. In other words, don't apply for the position at the DCCC if you're a Republican. You might get hired, but you can kiss your hopes of working for the GOP good-bye. Likewise, if you worked as an intern for a Democrat on Capitol Hill and then apply to the NRCC, you likely will be passed over.

One last thing to keep in mind about the Hill committees is that they're starved for interns and temporary staff during election years. Now, many of those positions get filled for the summer, with college students on break. So, what should you do? See if you can take a semester off to work at one of the committees. Granted, you might not be able to, but for those who can, working during the fall or spring is a great way to get your foot in the door.

TWO SKILLS TO SUCCEED

Finally, we want to address two skills that would serve you well if you're applying for any position above an intern at either the national committees or the Hill or governors committees. As opposed to a Capitol Hill office, party committees function much more like a company. There are departments and divisions; there are layers of management; and there's a chairperson, or CEO, overseeing it all. This corporate structure will require you to approach a job at the committees in a somewhat different way than you would on Capitol Hill.

1. Be a Specialist

Long gone are the days when someone could be just a "campaign expert." The jack-of-all-trades role doesn't exist anymore in politics, especially campaign politics. Some of the committees want specialists to fit certain roles within a given department. So, if you apply for an internship or a full-time position at one of the committees without much relevant experience in a specific field, you may get rejected. For example, the website of the NRCC has an internship application form that asks applicants to choose a "First Branch Preference." They are finance, political, communications, treasury, legal, executive, digital, data, member services, and research.

Now, as an intern, you wouldn't be expected to come in with much expertise in any of these fields. The committee needs warm bodies to do the grunt work. You *should* pick a field that interests you since you will learn a lot about it. But the fact that even interns must pick a field at all goes to show what an applicant for a job should expect.

This is an important difference with Capitol Hill, where you don't necessarily need to be an expert to land an entry-level position. As you move up the Hill, you will choose either policy or communications, and the expertise will soon follow. Not so on the committees. They need someone who knows what they are doing from day one.

So, how do you get that experience?

Hill committees thrive on hiring applicants who come from the political campaign world, private sector, or Capitol Hill. In other words, you get your experience elsewhere, then take your talents to the committee. Obviously, this means that your chances of landing a job as a fresh-out-of-school applicant are slim, but not impossible. Particularly if you're still in school, it's in your best interest to gain some experience—any experience—in one of the fields on the committee's list. Course work helps, but doesn't cut it as experience. Instead, you will want to volunteer, intern, or even work part-time at a committee organization or campaign that could provide you with the relevant experience.

The specialist angle is also useful to keep in mind if, say, you're a Hill staffer who wants to get more involved on the partisan campaign side. The Hill committees as well as the national committees are ideal locations for Hill staffers looking to advance their political career elsewhere. And as we said above, many colleagues of ours jumped back and forth between the committees and the Hill. It all depends on what you enjoy and how you want to advance your career.

2. An Office of Politics

A colleague of ours who worked in the digital space of one of the Hill committees passed along this story, which we believe is extremely useful.

> *When I first started, I wish someone had told me how the Hill committees are so political. That sounds odd since I worked in politics, but I didn't expect the politics that took place inside the office. As an example, I was responsible for securing the necessary budget for our digital group. But everyone in the building was going after the same finite amount of money. The rule is that if you're winning your budget battle, someone is losing theirs. That's how things go, particularly at a nonprofit. The*

*problem I faced is that digital was a brand-new space. Even if
the older veterans understood the importance of building up our
digital space, they didn't care come budget time. Besides, those
veterans were better connected than I was. They knew how to
play the budget game far better than me. It didn't matter how
persuasively or eloquently I made my case. Every time I fought
for a budget, I was going up against a buzz saw. It made me
upset and dispirited.*

*Eventually I realized that the problem wasn't that no one
understood the importance of digital. The problem was that
I didn't know how to play the game. I had to build my own
coalition, a network of allies, in the office, who would fight for
me come budget time. So, every day I would take a lap around
the building, poking my head into offices and asking if the occu-
pant needed anything from digital. In time, I had built up my
network and no small amount of favors that I was ready to call
in when the moment came. It was very Machiavellian, because
I was angling to take their budget away. But it worked. I started
to win my budget battles . . . and someone else lost theirs.*

As we mentioned earlier, the national committees and the Hill
committees function much more like a business than Capitol Hill.
What our colleague relates above would sound familiar to anyone who
has ever fought for a budget in a company. But for someone who has
never worked in the corporate world, or who has only worked on the
Hill, the Machiavellian nature of internal office politics can come as a
shock. You can expect to be underhanded and backstabbing with the
other side, your political opponents. But your colleagues?

That's one way to look at it. There's another way, as our colleague
explained. He said that there are two types of people in the Hill committees: coalition builders and jerks. The jerks barge in and demand.
Sometimes they get results, but mostly they make enemies. The coalition builders form relationships and alliances. They don't gain friends
by selling snake oil or making promises they can't keep. They fulfill

their end of the bargain. That their friends also do as they promised is what makes the whole system work.

Machiavellian isn't exactly the right term, since Machiavelli was concerned about how one person assumes total power. That's not what we're talking about. Rather, we're talking about how you will have to play the political game to do your job. Forging alliances and doing favors are how Washington works. We want you to be fully aware of this going in, as our colleague wished he had been. But it's no more complicated than being a good colleague, making friends, and helping when someone is in need. Yes, you expect a favor in return, but when it comes, that is simply someone else being a friend to you.

A MULTITUDE OF OPTIONS

The alternate routes we discussed in the chapter are meant to show you the many ways one can get started in politics. Even though we've focused this book on Capitol Hill, the beauty of our constitutional system is that democracy flourishes across this great country. You don't need to be in the center to make a difference. Nor do you even need to work in government. The various national and state party committees allow you to be an integral part of the democratic process at its most extreme. From conducting presidential debates to registering new voters, the party committees and campaigns serve as the laboratories for our democracy. Elections are what power our republic. They are the instruments through which we hold our elected representatives accountable and voice our approval . . . or disgust. To be at one of the party committees is to be in the very nerve center of the electoral system.

You should also look at these alternate routes as pathways to the Hill or diversions from it. There's no shame starting at the state or local level if your true ambition is Washington, DC. Nor is there shame in leaving DC to work at the legislature of your home state. You decide which mountain you want to climb. Make a difference where it matters most to you.

How They Climbed the Hill
MATT MOORE'S STORY

What makes us uniquely American is the ingrained notion that "you can start anywhere, and be anything." My parents stressed this continually, and I took it to heart. I feel pretty blessed and fortunate to have been born in a mobile home park in rural south Georgia and to go on to become the chairman of the South Carolina Republican Party.

You're reading a book by my fellow chairman on the Democratic side, Jaime, a guy who also came from nothing. Perhaps that's why we worked well together—when we weren't trying to beat the snot out of each other at the ballot box. He asked me to tell you a little bit about state politics, since I spent most of my career at the state level. Now I'm spending too much time in Washington, and Jaime is in South Carolina. Go figure.

Growing up, I didn't have much of an interest in politics. At Georgia Tech, I studied engineering and completed my senior project on the power of big data. I never attended a College Republicans meeting. Logically, I expected to go into engineering, but something pulled my gaze toward Georgia's State Capitol in Atlanta, a building known to locals as the Gold Dome, for obvious reasons. What was it?

My grandfather, a man who worked with his hands his whole life, took me to the famous "Wild Hog Supper" every year during college, given his service on a local power company's board. A kickoff to Georgia's annual legislative session that has taken place for more than fifty years, the supper brings together every politico in the state. It's a fun, raucous evening, where normal people like my grandfather could brush up against governors, lobbyists, and state officials.

What intrigued me at the time—and still intrigues me to this day—is the direct link between the people and their local government leaders. Outside of election season, national politicians don't spend much time with their constituents. We know national officeholders, if we know them at all, as faces on a screen.

But state politics is different, much more like national politics must have been around the time of Lincoln, who would greet the public at the White House. There's more intimacy at the state level, more of a sense that the person you vote for (or against) is also your neighbor whom you might run into at the grocery store. Such local elected officials care deeply because they have skin in the game—and no one wants to be embarrassed in the produce aisle, or harm their reputation in the community.

Whatever the reason, instead of searching for high-paying engineering jobs, I applied to be an intern for the Georgia Governor's Office, a job that paid seven dollars an hour. I got it, and within three months, I was asked to join a gubernatorial campaign as a software engineer. So I ended up an engineer anyway! Two years later, I was in Washington working for the Republican Governors Association, but didn't love "the Swamp." For all of the reasons I enjoy state politics, I often dislike Washington politics—it is too impersonal. In late 2007, I met then South Carolina Governor Mark Sanford, who was looking for political help, and that's how I ended up leaving Washington and moving to South Carolina.

Since then, I have worked on nearly every major campaign in South Carolina over the last ten years. I have worked on the smallest school board campaign and on the most contentious gubernatorial race. I'm very proud that a few small-town, local candidates I helped to win "way back when" are now serving in the US Congress. I have immersed myself in the state of South Carolina, its geography, and its people. I even met my wife there! That's one thing those powerhouse consultants in DC often forget: people vote their families, their wallets, their schools, and their safety. Numbers on a spreadsheet simply cannot take the place of knowing someone.

If you're interested in the game of politics, I implore you to spend some time working at the state level. You will usually learn more tactical know-how working on a campaign for school board than working on a presidential campaign. Politics is the study of people and what motivates them. Know the people you want to motivate, and learn every skill possible.

I will also second what Jaime and Amos have to say about the power of a state network. I met Governor Sanford in 2007 and stayed connected with him through his downfall and eventual return to the US Congress. I'm also blessed to know the other South Carolina Republicans who are playing starring roles at the national level. But setting that aside, I wouldn't have been so close to the governor—or those other influential South Carolinians—had I stayed in Washington. By getting out of Washington and into an early primary state, I also had a front row seat to seeing how and why Donald Trump won the presidency in 2016.

Developing an in-state network of friends and activists led me to becoming chairman of the South Carolina Republican Party, which is where I met Jaime and why you're reading me now. In May 2013, my friend Chad Connelly had just won reelection as the state chairman. But he had an offer for another position and called me in to talk about his potential successor. We bandied a few names about until Chad looked at me and said, "What about you?"

Well, what about me? A kid from America's rural South who spent most of his career in state politics and found a way to succeed. Now, what about you?

—**MATT MOORE,** consultant, Republican strategist and partner at First Tuesday Strategies; and chairman, South Carolina Republican Party, 2013–2017

CHAPTER 7

STAYING ON THE TRAIL

This is the chapter you don't want your parents—or spouse or loved ones—to read. This is the chapter that's all about the corrupting, immoral, and soul-sucking nature of work in politics and government. This is the chapter that warns you about how easy it is to fall victim to the Washington sirens (of the ancient Greek variety): the naked ambition, the pursuit of power, and the tantalizing temptations around every corner. Everything in this chapter should scream to you: abandon all hope ye who enter here.

Nah, we're only joking—mostly. You can certainly show your loved ones this chapter.

The truth is that we wanted to write a chapter that speaks to keeping one's career in politics on the right path. Chances are you have some notion that politics is a rough-and-tumble activity for all involved, from the president of the United States down to the city hall staffer. And chances are you've heard of a politician or a political operative who has had a spectacular fall from grace. Financial scandals, sex scandals, social media scandals—the examples we could cite would fill this book.

But do you know what other industry has scandals of this sort? All of them. Committing fireable offenses while on or off the job isn't unique to Washington, Congress, or government work in general. Derailing your career because of a stupid tweet or Facebook post happens all the time in every sort of business you can imagine. "Don't send a stupid tweet" isn't the sort of insider knowledge that you should expect from two seasoned former Hill staffers. You certainly didn't need to buy this book to learn that. Rather, we're going to focus on the traps and pitfalls that are (mostly) unique to Capitol Hill and political work. Our aim is to give you this information now so that you don't have to learn it on the job; to highlight the temptations and struggles that will confront you before they confront you; and to help you better discern and identify colleagues whose conduct is best avoided.

Still, don't send a stupid tweet.

DO THE RIGHT THING

Congressional staffers are held to a different standard, as they should be. For starters, your salary comes from taxpayers. This detail is more than just a minor point. It is everything. The American people are the reason you can pay your rent; pay down your student loan debt; buy groceries; and even get the occasional beer (or two) at happy hour. This fact won't (and shouldn't) dominate your thoughts and actions all day long. After all, your first priority is to your immediate boss, who has been elected to represent the best interests of his or her constituents— the American taxpayers.

Why is it important to remember the public nature of Hill work? Because it should be the foundation upon which you build your career in government. You are a public servant. Your party affiliation and your work for the House or Senate, state or district, committee or office—all of that is secondary to the reality of your situation, which is that you are there to serve the public's interest. This fact should be your North Star, the shining point that guides you in the dark hours, when your conscience and ethics are put to the test. Should you do this? Should you do that? You won't always know the right answer. But at such moments think about constituents back in your state or district. What would they think about this decision or that one? Could you explain your actions with a clear conscience? Such mental calculations have a way of clarifying the choice before you.

The other main reason politics isn't like other industries is because it is a direct by-product of our representative democracy. Again, don't let this mundane and obvious point obscure the deeper truth. You have a job because the American people are good enough to send their money to support our government and those who represent them in our government. For many who work in government and on Capitol Hill, they *also* have a job because someone received more votes than another person. Even if you work on a committee, and thus not directly for a member, you still owe your position to those who got theirs because of the democratic process. What's more, there are a whole bunch of dedicated, talented people backed by millions of dollars whose sole focus is making sure that your boss isn't elected next time.

Elementary, right? But look at it this way: Every two or six years, millions of dollars are spent to put you out of a job. Yes, you, the lowly staffer who's been answering phones for a year. Sure, you don't *have* to see it this way. You could tell yourself that all that money and attention are focused on your boss and have nothing to do with you. But if your boss goes, you go. And there's a flip side: If you do something that makes it harder for your boss to beat all those millions of dollars, you go as well. The margin for error is so razor thin in government precisely because the stakes are so high. It's hard enough to get (re)elected; no one wants a staffer whose actions have made it harder. Put another way, you are replaceable—and you will be replaced if you put your boss in any kind of jeopardy.

As we move into the dos and don'ts of this chapter, it's best to keep these two realities of Hill (or government) work in mind. First, you are a public servant whose livelihood comes courtesy of millions of nameless people, your countrymen and countrywomen. As such, do the right thing. Second, you are now part of the democratic process at its most extreme. When millions of dollars are spent to sway a few thousand votes, do you believe that anyone will have the least bit of patience for a staffer's mindless mistake? So, do the right thing.

Now, let's discuss the common traps or mistakes that staffers and sometimes even members fall into and explain how to avoid them.

Trap #1: I Just Work Here

Older people may recognize the word *macaca*. But if you're younger, here's a bit of electoral trivia. In 2006, Senator George Allen of Virginia was running for reelection against Jim Webb, the former secretary of the navy. During a campaign stop, Allen diverted from his traditional stump speech to point at a person in the crowd recording him. The senator joked to the crowd that this person worked for Webb and had been following him around with his camera. The kid with the camcorder caught the whole thing on tape. He filmed Allen referring to him—a dark-skinned person—as *macaca*.

The fallout that hit Allen was immense. Just google *macaca*. Without rehashing all the twists and turns the story took, the central question was whether Allen had used a racist slur to describe the cameraman. And *that* was what Allen had to talk about and explain for the remainder of the race, not his tenure and record as an incumbent senator and former governor of Virginia. Webb won.

Both of us were on the Hill at the time and followed the story closely. Everyone in Congress was glued to it. It was such a fascinating—and terrifying—moment for anyone who worked in politics. Campaigns have been sending "trackers" to follow their opponents on the trail since the dawn of American democracy. There's nothing quite like a video to show what words can only describe. And the only video of Allen's "*macaca* moment" came from Webb's tracker. The media wasn't even there.

Today we have accepted the new fact of political life: Anyone can be watching—and recording—and has access via social networks to millions of people. Back in 2006, however, it was a brave new world, and Allen was one of the first to feel its impact. This new world, however, isn't solely focused on candidates and members of Congress. It has come to include nearly anyone who works for those candidates and members. That means you. At any moment, someone might be watching and recording you.

So, who cares if someone films you singing karaoke at happy hour? Well, no one, and we don't want to make you paranoid that shadowy campaign operatives will be following you around. But we do want to make you aware that what you do reflects on your boss. The idea that when you leave work you are "off the clock" and, thus, excused from serving your boss must be smashed.

If you get caught doing something stupid, there's a chance you could lose your job.

All employees at some level represent the companies for which they work, but no employees reflect their bosses as much as political staffers. A company employee getting caught doing something stupid probably won't impact the company's bottom line all that much (of course there are exceptions). But a political staffer? Again, not all stupidities are equal, but when you're dealing with an office of a dozen or so people, even the tiniest screwup can shake the entire operation. What's more, as you'll read below when we get to the media, what you say can be, and will be, twisted by your political opponents as if you were speaking on behalf of your boss.

For example, say you tweet how much you hate program "X" and wish it was ended. From your perspective, this was a personal comment. But to anyone who's looking to criticize your boss, it can be twisted to mean "Rep. Doe's staffer says program 'X' should be eliminated." Suddenly, you're the center of the political world—that is, until you get fired.

Which is why you should never allow yourself the comfort of being "off the clock." You aren't a random employee—you're a representative of an elected official. Act like it. At all times.

Now comes the scary part. Every campaign season, the two sides in an election (or multiple sides in a primary) scour every shred of information they can find on their opponents. This is what's called opposition (or oppo) research. It can be an ugly business for the candidates and their families. Staffers *usually* don't find themselves caught up in the other side's oppo research. So, don't worry too much about deleting every Facebook picture of you being stupid in college (but try to get as many as you can). There are exceptions, and those usually depend on the position of the staffer and the type of indiscretion. An LA with a DUI on her record isn't going to see her mug shot splattered over the internet, but a press secretary, legislative director, or chief of staff? The higher the position of the staffer, the more valuable the embarrassment is to the other side.

We don't tell you this to scare you away or induce paranoia. We want you to be smart. Realize that as a staffer you are part of something much bigger than yourself. This means that what you do from now on, both in and out of the office, should only be done after you've answered one question: how will this reflect on my boss?

Trap #2: Do You Know Whom I Work For?

Newly minted staffers and interns perform a specific ritual when they head out for drinks after work: They all refuse to remove their ID badges. It's kind of endearing. Head out to any bar around the Capitol right around happy hour, and you'll see the hordes of young staffers doing what young staffers do when the workday is done: drinks in hand, coats off, ties loose, sleeves rolled up, but never without the all-important photo badge dangling from those metal-beaded lanyards. We performed this ritual in our day. You'll do it too.

Why? Well, the noble answer is that you're proud to be a staffer. You know what it took to get that badge, and you're going to wear that piece of plastic until it falls apart. That's mostly true. The more honest answer is that badge means you're Somebody. You're Important. Sure, you might just be answering phones and opening mail, but so is everyone else out on Bucket-of-Beers night. It feels good to wear that badge because everyone is wondering the same thing: *whom* does she work for?

Ah, and that's the special glue that binds politicos together. The all-important question, one that is asked no matter how high up the Hill ladder you have climbed: *Whom* do you work for? It's the principal conversation starter in Washington, DC—and in every state captiol we imagine.

This sense of importance is very much a part of our unique little community. Work on the Hill for a while, and you'll get over the badge-wearing ritual. Leave that for the recent graduates. But you never get over the exhilarating sense of how close you are to real power. Rise high enough, and you'll start to wield some of that power yourself. Now we're talking. Now you don't even need the badge. Now everyone knows who *you* are.

Unflattering? You bet. Understandable? Absolutely. It so happens that politics is power in its truest form. There's nothing shameful about feeling its draw. That pull to work in DC or a state capital is the gravitational force of power. These are places where things happen (sometimes). These are places where stuff gets done (or not). Your motivations are likely pure, but your aim is to change the world, and to do that you have to go to places of power and influence.

There's nothing shameful in reveling a little bit in your proximity to this power. You work at the epicenter of human power on Earth. Enjoy your place in history and the fact that you are a part of Big Things. As Abraham Lincoln said, "Nearly all men can stand adversity, but if you want to test a man's character, give him power."

Unfortunately, power corrupts. Power can turn a decent human being into a monster. You are not immune from this truth. Power is a trap, for all the reasons that humankind has discovered over the centuries. It is a trap particularly for political staffers because it is illusory. To be blunt: You don't have any power. No one elected you to do anything. Read that sentence again. Let it sink in. Ready? Okay, because even if you don't have any real power of your own, you will still wield power. What you acquire is the power to speak on behalf of your member. In practice, this turns out to be very similar to having that power yourself. Similar, not the same.

Yet the effect on one's ego can be as if you had the power yourself. After all, when you tell someone to jump and the response is "how high?" does it matter if you're speaking on behalf of your boss? The person did what you asked. In any case, you can see how a staffer can get used to being obeyed; to having orders put into action; to making those beneath the staffer tremble in his or her presence. These attributes of power expose how fragile our morals can be when given a little bit of it.

When Amos's talk with a reporter resulted in a segment on the nightly news—that's power. When Jaime worked the back channels of an important floor vote and got a bill passed—that's power. When Amos could ignore a call from the *New York Times*—that's power. When Jaime spoke to a room full of elected officials and they *listened*— that's power. When either of us sat down with our member and advised him on a specific course of action—action he followed—that's power.

We like to think that we never abused the power we were given. We want to believe that we never talked down to an intern because he or she was *just an intern*. But we are human, and so are you.

It's okay to make those minor mistakes. Work needs to get done, and if you need to throw your weight around a bit, that's part of the job. But we have seen a lot of staffers forget the fundamental truth about power: They don't have any. And the thing about the Hill is that a staffer who steps over the line will feel the consequences. Maybe not right away, but eventually. Why? Because in the end the Hill is a community, and it only functions when its inhabitants can work with each other. An aberrant staffer, someone whose pride in his or her own importance affects everyone nearby, is like a discordant note in a piece of music. It is noticed, and not in a good way.

For this reason, the arrogant staffer doesn't last long. Pride will lead to carelessness, then sloppiness. Maybe the staffer can get by because the tactics lead to results, but eventually he or she will overstep. Pride before the fall. The worst thing that can happen to you as a staffer is to lose the trust of your boss. When that happens, no amount of illusory power in the world will save your job. And members aren't too fond of staffers who act like they were the ones who got elected.

We offer this discourse on power and human nature because we want you to enter the Hill prepared, not because we think you're about to turn into a tyrant. We want you to know not only how those feelings of pride can easily turn into arrogance, but also why. We want you to be aware of the temptations that await you as you climb the Hill, so that you can recognize them in yourself and others.

Trap #3: No Worries, I Got This

This trap is very much an offshoot of our discussion on power but is much more practical. The simple fact is that the caricature of the tyrannical Hill staffer is rare. As we said, those people don't last on the Hill. It's much more likely that you'll abuse your power in a far more innocent and excusable way. But that doesn't mean you won't get in trouble for it. Even a justified overstep can lead to severe consequences, as Jaime found out.

The 2006 midterm election was a very good day for the Democratic Party, which recaptured both the House and the Senate. It was also historic, because it led to Nancy Pelosi becoming the first woman Speaker of the House. There were several driving issues in the 2006 election, and under Speaker Pelosi the new Congress would consider all of the issues. Now running the whip operation for Majority Whip James Clyburn, Jaime was tasked with garnering the support of Democrats in the House. On one particular bill, a group of House Democrats decided to oppose the legislation because the language was not strong enough. The vote was extremely close. Jaime spent days talking to the members, soliciting their support for the measure. In particular, he spoke with a staffer for one influential member who was a nay on the bill. If Jaime could turn that member's vote to a yea, other holdouts would likely follow. During the discussion, Jaime asked what that staffer's boss needed to see in the bill. The staffer proposed suggested modifications. Jaime assumed that the staffer was speaking on behalf of the member but never asked. He took the offer to Clyburn, explaining how they could turn nay votes into yeas. The Democratic leadership, taking Jaime's words as gospel, made the changes to the bill. Everything was in order. Jaime had done his job, and his boss had proved himself as an effective majority whip.

Yet the member remained opposed to the bill. What had happened? The answer was simple: Jaime didn't do his due diligence. He didn't verify with the member or the staffer that this was a commitment and that the staffer could speak on behalf of the member.

Jaime's mistake was not double-checking. He let his excitement over a proposed (but imaginary) deal cloud his judgment. It was a big mistake, and not just because it jeopardized the bill. Clyburn had won his position as majority whip after a heated internal debate. These bills were Clyburn's big tests—which meant that it was Jaime's and the rest of the office's big tests. Could they rise to the occasion?

Then this happened. The humiliation was very real and very personal to Jaime, who felt he had let everyone down.

This story is an example of the way power dynamics work on the Hill. Information gets passed between staffers and between members and staff, and the value of that information depends on the authority of the one passing it. Members certainly meet with each other, but in the day-to-day workings of the Hill, the bulk of the work falls to staffers. Not only is it important for you to be aware of your own power and authority, but you must also know the power and authority of the staffer across the table, computer screen, or other end of the phone. Being conscious of the power you and your colleagues wield is a big part of performing your job well.

Trap #4: We're Just Friends

Here's the thing: Capitol Hill is a very small place (statehouses are even smaller). You'll notice how small the moment you're shown your "workstation." Crammed cheek by jowl next to your coworkers isn't the most ideal work environment, but, then again, you're usually too busy to notice. You will, however, get to know your coworkers and colleagues very well. Too well, in some cases. Hill work is emotional and stressful, and tempers often run hot. The Hill is also a very social place, where your colleagues are likely to become your friends—sometimes the only friends you will see for weeks at a time. Emotional, close-knit, long hours—you can see where this is going.

We're not puritans, and we don't expect you to be either. We want you to be smart and heed the advice of two people who have seen every variety of romantic political relationships. Our advice: Avoid them. There's no reason to get into a long diatribe about romantic entanglements to make the obvious point that sleeping with your coworkers rarely ends well. For all the details we stated above—intimate working conditions, small community, hot tempers—the last thing you want to do is add a layer of personal complication to your life.

This is not to say that relationships of any kind should be avoided. Go on dates, have fun, be young. Just try to do it outside the office and preferably off the Hill. Otherwise, everyone—and we mean everyone—in your office will know your business.

Trap #5: When Opportunity Knocks, Answer!

A company that has as much internal movement and turnover as Capitol Hill would cease to function. Every two years, a sizable number of the occupants of the House and Senate seats change due to the election or retirement, leaving the old staffers out in the cold as a new office moves in. Meanwhile, continual staffer movement—between offices and chambers—requires a steady stream of new hires. That Congress doesn't come to a screeching halt is a testament to the veteran staffers who know what they're doing. It's a minor point, but we should never take for granted the smooth transition from one Congress to the next.

All this internal change means that at any given moment there are several job openings on the Hill. If you're in an entry-level position, such as a staff assistant, the temptation to jump at these opportunities will be strong. You've only been in your current office a few months, but why not throw your hat in the ring? What's the danger of trying to climb the Hill? After all, isn't that the point of this book?

Don't. If you were at an entry-level position at a corporation for a few months and a higher position opened at another corporation, would you go for it? After you consider that your potential new boss will likely speak to your old boss—who now knows you're looking around—you probably wouldn't. It's also unlikely that you'd get the position after only a few months of experience, because who wants to hire someone who's probably going to leave in a few months?

It's no different on the Hill. The hit to your career could be even worse. Why? One word: loyalty. There is no more valuable commodity in politics than loyalty. When you join an office, you are expected to show loyalty to your member. We don't just mean a superficial loyalty that an employee has for the company that pays him or her. We mean loyalty in the very strict, very serious sense. Chances are you've never experienced such loyalty in other types of work. Those were just jobs after all.

The loyalty we're talking about commits you to the success of your member. It commits you to a tenure of service that should be able to weather the "better opportunity." If it doesn't, you're not in the right line of work. If you can't give yourself to the job, look elsewhere. If you're squeamish about doing all you can to protect and promote your member, don't go to the Hill. Because in the end, loyalty is how you build your career; it's how you climb. A staffer who shows loyalty will be more highly prized (and recruited) than the one who might be smarter and more skilled, but whose loyalty is suspect. Intelligence and skills are in abundance, especially in Washington, DC. Loyalty is scarce. If you know anything about economics, you know that the scarcer the resource, the more valuable it is.

But a staffer who's only out for himself or herself—who reveals that career interests trump those of the member—is a staffer who will soon be without a member to give his or her loyalty to. Like the arrogant, power-hungry staffer, opportunists don't last long on the Hill. It only takes one or two quick job changes for the rest of the Hill to put you on its watch list. The list is simple: It says this person can't be trusted. Why would an office bring in someone and let the staffer see the inside of a political operation, when it knows this person always has one foot out the door?

Patience is a virtue on the Hill. There are exceptions, but you don't get to climb higher without paying your dues. Great opportunities show up all the time, but you must have the patience and discipline to let them go. Believe us, we know the difficulties and frustrations of those lower-end positions. The salary isn't that great; you do a lot of work for little reward; and you feel that you're better than the responsibilities you have.

But here's the good news. No one who is any good on the Hill stays in an entry-level position for very long. If you follow our advice from earlier in the book about how to get ahead, you will be noticed. We also hasten to add that we aren't against advancing your career. Far from it. We tell you this because we want you to advance up the Hill as high as you want. That's not to say you should never transition from one office to another. It happens all the time. How else would you climb the Hill? But you must have patience. Advancement will come.

And come quickly. Most Hill careers last fewer than ten years. Neither of us was on the Hill even that long, and we climbed to its highest levels. Sure, luck has a little bit to do with it, but we also never felt like we "lucked" into any job beyond our first one. The first one is almost always lucky, because of how hard the job is to get. After you're in, it's up to you to stay in. Failure to advance is almost never because of bad luck. It's almost always because of the person you see in the mirror. So, we repeat: patience.

In the meantime, you will be learning something that is more valuable than the job you have: You will learn how to be loyal. You will see how those ahead of you in the office got there, and you will start to emulate them. *How* do they serve their boss? *Where* are their priorities day-to-day? *When* do they leave for another position?

You will also quickly grow a genuine love for your office and its staff. And we do mean love. We hesitate to compare Hill work to battle, but allow us this indulgence. In battle, the bonds that are forged between soldiers last forever. No one else will ever understand what a soldier and his or her fellows experienced in the field. It's an unbreakable bond, a shared experience that will always connect them, no matter how long they go without seeing each other.

On the Hill, you and your coworkers will go through very difficult times. There will be very late nights—nights that never end—and extremely stressful situations, where the outcome seems hopeless and all you have to get through the day is each other. Your elders will call these moments "character building," and they certainly are that. You will learn more about yourself than you ever knew. But we always felt that the true value of these moments was in the relationship building, the bonds of friendship that only exist when people have gone through the ringer together. And these are the relationships that will last the rest of your life. Years after you leave the Hill, you will meet up with an old colleague, and you will never laugh harder over a memory that, at the time, was a horrible experience. No one listening in will have the faintest idea what's so funny about such an ordeal. But you and your old colleague know, and that's what matters.

If any of that makes sense, you already know a little bit about loyalty. And if you know a little about loyalty, you'll know why it's sometimes best not to answer when opportunity knocks.

WHERE TO FIND HELP

The government entities we've talked about in this book—the Hill, committees, statehouses, and the like—don't have traditional human resource departments. What the Hill does have are committees in both chambers that function like an HR department. These are where a staffer would go to report an incident of sexual, disability, racial, or ethnicity related discrimination, abuse, and harassment. These departments are called the Committee on House Administration and the Senate Committee on Rules and Administration. You will know these committees because they handle a lot of the administration details of your employment. The Office of Compliance also handles reports of abusive or discriminatory behavior. These committees are there for a reason. Use their services whenever you need assistance or advice about your benefits or employer, or protection against discrimination.

ABOUT THE MEDIA . . .

According to a 2015 study from the Pew Research Center, roughly sixty-eight hundred news personnel cover Congress. That's more than the entire Senate staff. No other industry is as scrutinized as much as politics, whether we're talking about Washington, a state capital, or a city hall. Working in politics means you work under a microscope— although in this case, the microscope is a swarm of eager, ambitious reporters. Their goals can sometimes (but not always) be at odds with your goal: to protect and advance the interests of your boss.

This is as it should be. Believe us, you'll develop a strong love-hate relationship with the media while you are a staffer. Yet there's a reason the press is mentioned in the First Amendment: It serves an integral part of our democracy. The Founding Fathers understood that governments tend to hide or obscure information from the public. Working in government, you'll learn why this is the case. It's not always a bad thing— some information is classified for a reason. Other information, such as details of a bill or how a particular member will vote, is withheld to effect a desired outcome. This obfuscation is in the interest of the elected official behind it, but that doesn't mean it's not in the public's interest to know. Reporters rarely will bury a scoop to satisfy a politician's agenda.

When you're starting on the Hill, there's a simple rule to follow with the media: Don't talk to them unless it is your job to do so. It's unlikely you'll be in a position where you would talk formally with a member of the media, although being on the press side might lead to some interaction. When Amos was a new staffer on the House Energy and Commerce Committee, it was a fireable offense to speak with the media, unless you were in the press shop, in which case it was your job. We could sugarcoat the reasons behind this rule, but we're not going to. The fact is that you don't know how to talk to the media. Not yet anyway. In time, you'll learn the basics, but when you're a new staffer, accept that you're wholly unprepared for it.

As a staffer, you must understand that whatever you say to a reporter will be printed as if it comes from the member. Unless you're speaking to a reporter on background or off the record, everything you say is liable to be published. Everything. Reporters swarm the Hill every hour of the day looking for someone to talk to. They *want* to talk to you; yes, you, the lowly staffer. Why? Because you know something the reporters don't. Just working in a Hill office grants you access to information that any reporter would want to have. Reporters worth their salt aren't going to try to find a member of Congress to talk to; they know it's a dead end. But a staffer, especially a new one who's a bit wet behind the ears? You're journalistic gold, because they can use all their reporter tricks to get you to talk. Then before you know it, you're reading your own words the next day (or later that day), only you're now a "congressional source."

Oh, we know. You won't talk. You'll be able to tell when a reporter is fishing for dirt. Will you? Will you know whether the guy who just struck up a conversation with you at the bar is a reporter? Will you be able to resist the charm of a reporter whose trick is to get you talking about your own importance—or your own frustrations? Don't underestimate the lengths a reporter will go to get you to spill the tiniest, most insignificant piece of information.

"I befriend people, and I betray them publicly," said one veteran reporter in a story about the fall of a staffer who couldn't resist giving information. Understand that Washington, or any state capital, is a place that feeds off information. The moment you gain access to Capitol Hill, you become a potential conduit of information for the media hordes stuck on the outside. Their job is to get you to talk. They will feel absolutely no remorse tricking you into telling them something useful.

However, gain a little experience on the Hill, and you'll start to see the "love" side of the love-hate relationship. Remember, reporters are ravenous for information. That makes you valuable to them. Once you learn to keep your mouth shut, you will start to learn how to use the media to further your member's ends. You will want to take a reporter out for lunch or a drink. You'll probably even develop relationships with certain reporters that edge toward actual friendship—although it's more like "friendship." Because while reporters will accept being used to advance your member's interests, the good ones also know when to call in a favor. Quid pro quo—it's how things get done in Washington, DC.

A last word about the media: Even if you've advanced to the stage where you're a seasoned Hill staffer, one thing never changes. As a staffer, you never want to be the story. Put another way, you never want your presence in a story to be anything beyond the quote or tidbit of information you provided. If the story is about you, it's probably bad. You've become a distraction for the office, and distractions are discarded. It all goes back to what we said earlier in this chapter. Do the right thing, always. That way, you have nothing to worry about.

We want you to understand that power can be useful; it's how things get done. If you learn to use it properly, you will excel.

YOUR REPUTATION IS YOUR REAL POWER

After Jaime had joined the Podesta Group, he often assisted in the hiring of new team members straight from the Hill. Knowing that applicants had pursued a successful career in Congress told Jaime a lot about the type of people they were. It said they were loyal, hard-working, dedicated, and discreet. Hiring directly from the Hill also allowed Jaime to tap his old colleagues to get the real story about a potential hire. There are always two applicants in one: the applicant on the resume, and the applicant as a real person. Jaime wanted to know the real person, and the best way to do that was to talk to those who had worked with the applicant. In one case, an applicant the firm was considering checked all the right boxes. The person seemed perfect for the job. And then Jaime talked to this applicant's former colleagues on the Hill. The conversations rarely went beyond, "So we are considering hiring this applicant. . . ." To which came the reply, "Don't."

It turns out that this applicant had a horrible reputation from the Hill. And just like that, the applicant didn't get the job.

On the Hill, your reputation is your most important characteristic. In a world swimming in powerful people, your reputation is the only true power you have. It can open doors you never could have imagined and take you to heights previously undreamed. But it takes effort to build your reputation, as well as some good old-fashioned manners. In the end, everything we've told you about keeping your Hill career on the right track comes down to managing and protecting your reputation. Once you get a bad reputation, it is nearly impossible to continue your career—on the Hill or elsewhere.

In the tumult of the Hill, it isn't hard to lose one's way. You will occasionally become overbearing; you will even be mean at times. Recognize when you are and seek to make amends when you can. No one expects to be treated with kid gloves in politics, but no one ever has to tolerate cruelty. Use your power to get the job done, then use it to empower others. Never use it to advance your self-interests.

Treat others well, and you'll stay on the trail. Build your reputation—as a loyal, dependable, selfless worker—and it will take you as far as your ambition can climb.

How They Climbed the Hill
ELIZABETH MORRA'S STORY

Like many who work on the Hill, my first interest was journalism. At the University of Georgia, I worked as a reporter on the campus radio station. I remember driving through a snowstorm to Washington, DC to cover Ronald Reagan's second inauguration in January 1985. With tests the next day, I called in live reports from the frigid steps of Capitol Hill. I also interviewed a few members, including Senator Sam Nunn, and it was in his office that I found a pamphlet for summer internships. I picked it up, and decided to apply.

I'll never forget the grueling selection process. I was one of hundreds of students across Georgia vying for only a few internships on Nunn's staff. During an interview, I said that my ambition was to become a press secretary, even though I wasn't actually committed to a Hill career at this point. It just seemed like an appropriate answer for a journalism major like me. The question I got back was: "As President Nixon's press secretary during the Watergate scandal, what would you have done?" My answer couldn't have been that bad (I don't remember what I blurted out), because I got the internship.

Even though I loved my summer in Washington, I couldn't quite give up my broadcast ambitions. The way I saw it, it would be harder to transition from the Hill into broadcasting than vice versa. So I ended up in Panama Beach, FL, after graduation as an on-air news reporter. I jumped to Augusta, GA; then to Greensboro, NC; slowly inching my way closer to DC, but never quite making it all the way there.

After five years of a broadcast career, I met my husband, moved to DC, and began searching for my next job. I started to send resumes to jobs on the Hill as well as news channels. I remembered my past Washington summer fondly and wanted to make a career switch. But it proved difficult, as all career switches are. My old friends and colleagues from Nunn's office had moved on and I felt like I was starting from the very bottom—which I was. My five years as a journalist gave me some media experience, but I was just one of hundreds of journalists looking for a job on the Hill. Even my internship, which allowed me to say that I had Hill experience, didn't seem to be paying the dividends.

Then, a lucky break: I got connected to Senator Thad Cochran's staff director, who told me about a new in-house cable network that would cover Congress. The network would fall under Cochran's purview, meaning that it would be a congressional project and not a true media outlet, but I would oversee it. My job would be to keep the Hill informed on Hill business. Was I interested?

It was a completely different position from what I was seeking. I wouldn't be a "staffer" in the traditional sense, nor a press secretary. Rather I would operate on my own and cover the Hill as I saw fit. In other words, I would be doing it all, which I knew was a big responsibility from my reporting and producing days. But, I would be on the Hill. It would give me the opportunity to meet a number of key staffers and senators. I was grateful for the opportunity and took the job.

The job was a lot of work but provided good experience and exposure to key Hill people. I was a producer, reporter, and an anchor. I ran around the Hill with a camera team taping segments and rushed to make the segments suitable for viewing. The work itself was challenging, but the real concern was that we had no way of knowing who (if anyone) was watching. Were we making an impact? Were we useful at all? We had no idea.

But the job gave me my big opportunity. After a year, the communications director position opened up in Senator Cochran's personal office, and I was offered the job.

I immediately jumped at the chance to land the position on the Hill I most wanted and found myself in the center of the race for the next Majority Leader, when Cochran and Senator Trent Lott competed for the job. It was a very exciting time.

My experience taught me this: If your goal is the Hill, then get on the Hill. That's the best advice I can offer someone who is looking to do a mid-career switch into politics. If you're five or ten years out of college, you've earned the right to wait for the right position to come along . . . unless you're looking to get on the Hill. Then, you take what you can get and be happy with what you have.

When it comes to the Hill, there's a simple calculation: Do the job you have to get the job you want. I did. You can too.

—ELIZABETH MORRA, VP of Federal Affairs, University of North Carolina System

CHAPTER 8

PREPARING FOR THE
NEXT CHALLENGE

Most career advice books don't usually discuss the end of your career before you've had a chance to start one, but ours will. That's because you will likely spend most of your *career*—the work you do after college but before you retire—off the Hill. Estimates vary, but the average tenure of a Hill staffer is between three and six years. Senate staffers seem to hang on longer than House ones simply because of the six-year tenure of senators, but staffers with ten-plus years of experience are exceedingly rare. Nadeam Elshami, whom you met in chapter 2, is one of those exceptions. He belongs to an exclusive club of Hill staffers who logged more than twenty years.

Who cares? You spend a few years on the Hill, then you move on to something else. End of chapter, right? Not quite. The first thing to understand is *why* Hill careers are so short. We want you to pursue a Hill career with your eyes wide open, and we would be negligent if we didn't mention that eventually you'll probably want to leave. The second issue we'll discuss is how to go about leaving. There's a common misconception that everyone who leaves the Hill—member or staffer—is immediately offered a lobbyist contract. But lobbying is only one of several common career paths available to former staffers. And contrary to popular belief, lobbyist jobs don't just fall from the Washington, DC, sky.

Finally, it's important for you to understand that leaving the Hill is part of working on the Hill. What we mean is that many people start working on the Hill with the expectation that they won't stay for long. Since many know that they likely won't be a staffer in their sixties, it's incumbent on them to start preparing for departure sooner rather than later. We don't mean keeping your resume fresh and checking the job postings. We mean that the job you land off the Hill depends heavily on how well you did your job on the Hill.

In other words, we want you to be smart and strategic. For example, if you know you want to be a lobbyist, you should get to know policy, not communications. But if you want to be in PR, you should focus on communications. If you want to run your own political consulting firm one day or join a think tank, you should aim for a chief of staff or legislative director role. The opportunities available to you after spending a few productive years on the Hill will be wonderful and varied. You will be better positioned than your peers in other fields to take on responsibilities far beyond your age. You will be primed to carry on the level of activity and passion that powered you through those sleepless nights of an extended voting session. You will be prepared for great things.

WHY LEAVE?

We've spent the better part of this book extolling the virtues of being a Hill staffer, so why would we talk about leaving? Who would want to leave such a great, amazing, rewarding job? Answer: almost everyone. We did, after all. Doesn't that say something (bad) about the job itself? Yes and no. There's not a day that goes by for either of us that we don't miss our days as a staffer. The job itself remains one of the best experiences of our lives—and we have no doubt it will be the same for you, if you follow our advice. Yet there will come a point when you will want to leave, not because the job suddenly changes or becomes less rewarding, but because you change.

Before digging in deeper, let's look at some numbers. In 2013, the Congressional Management Foundation and the Society for Human Resource Management released a survey on Hill staffers that looked at job satisfaction and complaints, among other indicators. The survey found that 80 percent of staffers expressed overall satisfaction with the job—twice as high as in the general workforce. Moreover, *94 percent* said they keep at it because "they believe what they're doing is meaningful." Ninety-two percent said that they stay on the Hill because of "their desire to help people."

You can scour every industry on the globe and not find such remarkable numbers. They provide statistical proof that the things you've been reading in this book aren't a bunch of fluff and nonsense. You want passion; you want purpose; you want a reason to get up in the morning (or stay at work at night)? Then become a Hill staffer.

We've covered some of the downsides in previous chapters. Here are some additional details to consider.

Reason #1: The Money

Forty-six percent of staffers surveyed said that within a year they would look for a new job because of a "desire to earn more money." By now you know that living in Washington, DC, on an entry-level staffer salary is a tall order, so this stat shouldn't surprise you. Nevertheless, it is difficult to earn so little when your peers in other industries are earning so much—or least much more than you. Not only do they seem to have disposable income, but they also are—gasp!—saving. Meanwhile, you're considering driving for Uber or another ride-sharing company.

Despite the temptation to jump, consider sticking it out. The pay gets better as you rise through the ranks, and as we mentioned previously, you're never stuck in the same position for long on the Hill. Talent is recognized early and rewarded often, if not as quickly as some recent college graduates expect. Still, for many, the rate of promotion is too slow, the rewards of getting one too meager. For these staffers, leaving makes sense. If the sacrifice of building a Hill career is too great, nothing we can say will make you stay.

You will reach a limit, though. We both did. In 2007, Amos had been working on the Hill for five years. He was now married to Whitney, who was also a staffer, and their vision of their life together included children and living in Washington. Yet that vision was at odds with their income. They knew they wouldn't be able to afford the life they wanted if they both continued to work on the Hill. And they knew this despite both having reached the pinnacle of the Hill.

So, money became a major factor in Amos's decision to leave. He didn't want to. Amos still loved his job, particularly since he was in a position of authority. He knew that he could get any reporter in the country to return his call. As we said before, that's power. He could go home at night and watch the evening news, knowing that some of the featured stories were a direct result of his work.

Amos's example is one reason why we say that *you* will change. It's not that Amos couldn't live a very comfortable life with his family and stay on the Hill. But he and his wife had a vision for their life that was incompatible with what the Hill could provide.

Jaime wasn't all that different. We both grew up poor, but the level of Jaime's poverty far surpassed what Amos had experienced. Though he was by this point one of the highest-paid staffers on the Hill, Jaime's credit card and student loan debts kept him from using his money in the way he wanted: to help his family back home in South Carolina. Jaime did what he could, but he simply didn't make enough to spread it the way he wanted to. As a staffer with a law degree, Jaime had a good sense of how much money he wasn't making every year, compared to those who worked at law firms.

The economic collapse in 2008–2009 hit Jaime personally. His stepfather lost his job, and he and Jaime's mother were under threat of foreclosure on their home. By this time Jaime had left the Hill, and he was able to help financially. They could weather the bad times because Jaime had made the decision to seek a better-paying opportunity—not because he wanted better clothes or a nicer car. Because he wanted to give something back.

Being young sometimes calls for more "financial creativity." You can't afford anything, but you don't have many financial obligations. Besides, most of your peers are in a similar financial situation. Aside from paying off your loans and affording rent, your other major concern is having enough money for a degree of social life. In the grand scheme of things, that's still damn good. Yet your obligations grow the older you get, and a salary that kept a young professional in DC alive and happy can quickly turn into a liability. While Jaime appreciated how far he had come, he also knew there was money on the table, as they say—money his family obligations wouldn't let him ignore.

And that's the big point. You will grow up on the Hill, and in doing so, you may grow out of the Hill. Oh, you might return one day. We know several colleagues who move back and forth, but they do so on their terms. They have taken ownership of their careers and can command better salaries and leverage. Yet by building the first part of your career on the Hill, you will have obtained something that is invaluable in life: You will be in demand. You will recognize that the money you could earn as a successful former staffer more than makes up for the years you spent struggling to make ends meet. Those years can be tough, but there is a payoff.

Reason #2: The Mental Strain

Another stat from the staffer survey found that only about half of staffers (48 percent) felt they had time for a personal life. It bears repeating that having no personal life in your twenties sucks. Being a staffer isn't like being your typical nine-to-fiver. You're expected to be available at all times of the day, even on weekends. You won't see the chief of staff, legislative director, or press secretary going home early, and neither should you. And that's a key point. We can only assume that the half of respondents who felt like they had time for a personal life were those staffers who aren't interested in climbing the Hill anyway—or simply had no clue that success requires a measure of sacrifice.

But putting your personal life ahead of your career isn't always about having fun with your friends. (You will grow out of that.) The higher you climb on the Hill, the more the responsibilities of the job increase. Your free time will shrink in accordance with how high you rise. If you love your job (and we assume you will), these long hours are bearable. But they do take a toll, and not just on your social life. They can take a toll mentally, as well.

Some call it burnout. Work in politics long enough, and you start to live your life in cycles. Whether you are working on the Hill or in a campaign committee, the year takes on a predictable ebb and flow. Every other year, there is a national election; every four years, a presidential one. You'll quickly discover how much of the work in Congress depends on these campaign cycles. You must get this bill passed this year because next year is an election year. You must pass that bill because Congress will be on recess. And so on.

The pace can be relentless. Jaime recalls that in two years of working in the whip's office, he rarely went on a date. Then Speaker Pelosi was a driver of legislation, which meant Majority Whip Clyburn's office was on near constant alert. It wasn't uncommon for Jaime to be whipping votes on three major floor bills at the same time. You might not understand exactly what that means, but trust us—it's exhausting. During those years after the Democrats swept into the House, Jaime was working six, sometimes seven days a week.

Meanwhile, the predictability that comes with living your life by the clock of the election cycle carries its own kind of mental fatigue. "Here we go again" is the best way to describe it. For every major victory, there are dozens of little defeats and setbacks. Imagine a football game in which the offense spends the entire first quarter being pushed back against its own end zone. One big play propels your team fifty yards downfield, only for the slow withdrawal to begin again.

In American politics you never reach the end zone. There is always another election, another bill, another fight to be fought—and for most of these battles, you are being pushed back.

As with football, those big plays are thrilling. Unlike football, they also matter. If you love the game, you're happy to put up with the pushback just to experience that one big play. Stick around long enough, and you'll be part of more than a few. All the work you do to achieve one more—just one more big play—is well worth it. But what happens as you get older on the Hill is that enduring those little defeats starts to become harder and harder. It's not that you've grown cynical; more likely, you need a change. This mental exhaustion isn't universal. By the end Jaime was feeling burned out, but that's not how Amos felt at the end. He would've kept going if the money had been right.

We want you to be aware of the mental strain. Sometimes you need a break. Which doesn't mean that you'll leave the Hill or politics forever. It won't take long for you to miss the game. You'll be at your next job, perhaps making a lot more money, having a social life, and enjoying balance in your work and your personal life, and then you'll turn on the news and suddenly think, "You know, it wasn't so bad." So, it begins anew.

Reason #3: To Be Your Own (Wo)Man

To be a staffer is to assume your member's beliefs and opinions as your own. Even if you're lucky to work for a member whose ideals mirror yours, we can guarantee that you won't see eye to eye on all issues. And you won't be the first staffer to disagree with your member. It is simply unrealistic in the US political system to work for a legislator or executive and not have a difference of opinion from time to time. There are simply too many issues and too many competing interests.

The second thing to say is that you should cut your boss some slack. Your boss isn't taking a position to annoy you personally but is doing it (one hopes) because it's the best thing for his or her district and career. If you learn nothing else from our book, please remember that the only way things happen in Washington is through deliberation, collaboration, and compromise. The partisans on both sides hate that word—*compromise*. When they hear it, they think *sellout*. Those critics have the good fortune to snipe from the sidelines, because if they ever carried the weight of legislating on their shoulders, they would think differently. Achieving 218 votes in the House and 60 votes in the Senate to get legislation to the president is not a simple task, particularly when you have 535 members of Congress, all with their own experiences, ideas, and perspectives on any given legislative effort.

Also, be careful about criticizing your member for taking a position that is politically expedient. We all wish it didn't happen, but we live in a democracy. For a member to be of any value, he or she must be elected and reelected. Winning at the ballot box sometimes means a member must take positions that satisfy (or anger) a portion of the base. Maybe the issue that the member is against is your number one issue. We sympathize, but our best advice is to get over it or move on.

We don't mean to suggest that you must change your ideals. But we do guarantee that your perspective will change during your tenure. Why? Because as a staffer you will learn how government works. You will learn that politics is the intersection of ideas and action. You will learn why an idea you have believed in your whole life may be too impractical to put into action. You will learn that sometimes the idea that you are against is one avenue—perhaps the only avenue—to achieve a desired outcome. In short, you will mature as a political person while working on the Hill. You will see politics from both ends: the one where ideals reign and the other where legislation advances.

Most of all, your years as a staffer will sharpen your political acumen. You will no longer be the naive idealist; you will be a realistic idealist. You will come to see what is possible. And, yes, sometimes what is possible is something your superiors believe is impossible. You will become your own political person whose ideas have been forged in the crucible of the greatest experiment in democracy in history, the

US Congress. This experience will make your opinions worthwhile to your member, and suddenly you will be more than a staffer. You will be an advisor.

Both of us reached this level of the Hill. We not only had the title, we had the ear of our member. Our bosses *listened* to us. What does this have to do with leaving? Maybe nothing. Maybe you come to believe that your political skills and ideas are best used serving your member. Plenty of staffers make that choice. And plenty of members need excellent advisors. But there might come a point, as it did for us, when you realize it's time to be your own person. Even as an advisor, you're still a staffer. You still received zero votes. For some, that starts to become confining. Limiting. You come to believe that you can do more on your own than you can as a staffer.

When you come to this realization, you know it's time to leave. It's time to try your newly developed skills elsewhere. Your abilities have outgrown what you are able to accomplish as a staffer—and that's one of the most beautiful things about being a staffer. It encourages you to take what you have learned beyond the Hill, even beyond politics. The skills you have learned are more than political; they will serve you well wherever you go.

PREPARING FOR THE NEXT PEAK

So, you're ready to leave. What should you be doing to maximize your options off the Hill? It isn't so much what you should be doing now as what you should've been doing all along. This is why we're telling you about leaving the Hill before your career has even begun. Not only will our advice serve you in finding gainful employment off the Hill; it will also help you while you're still there. We admit that this section of the book is not as Hill-centric as other portions. The tips we provide probably would serve you well in any industry. That said, they are critical to your career if you want to leverage all you have done on the Hill.

Tip #1: Start Here—Meet Everyone

Perhaps the greatest long-term gift the Hill gives you is its people. We told you how important networking is to get your first internship or job on the Hill. Now we're telling you that it's even more important once you're there. If you're a shy, timid person, you need to learn how to break out of your shell. Politics is an industry of people. But some staffers who consider themselves policy wonks sometimes think they can simply put their head down, do their work, and that's enough. It's not.

The moment you step foot on the Hill, you should introduce yourself to everybody. Get into the habit of meeting new people, even if they're on the other side of the aisle. If you know you'll be working closely with them, go out for coffee or lunch. Learn who they are, not just about their day-to-day job. And remember names! Take each person's card, but don't throw it in a drawer somewhere. Yes, even in this digital age, business cards are important. They're physical reminders of a potential friend, ally, or mentor.

The world of politics is one of relationships. They're the grease that keeps the gears churning, and it's good to have friends scattered across the Hill. Things get done—when they get done at all—because of relationships, because of favors asked and granted. Everyone who succeeds on the Hill has their own network—their web of connections linking various elements of the Hill. If this sounds all too sleazy and Mafia-like, remember that politics is a game of relationships. It's not math, where the inputs match the output. It requires a very deliberate, very intimate human element if it's to work at all.

We're not asking you to be a transparent schmoozer. No one likes that person. Hill staffers are aware of the reason you're asking them out for coffee, but it takes more than coffee to form a true relationship. You will find yourself working with plenty of people you don't like personally (and who don't like you), but you'll be unlikely to go the extra mile for them—or they you. But a friend is different, and that's the type of relationship we're talking about. A friendship takes work, but once established, it rewards both parties.

Particularly when you leave the Hill and start to look for a job elsewhere, you will want to rely on the network you established and fostered for however long you were on the Hill. Your friends, some of whom don't even work on the Hill anymore, will be the ones who lead you toward your next job. They will also likely be the reason you obtain your next job. The recommendations they provide to your future employer are part of it; the other part is that your future employer will likely want to know *whom you know.* Not all jobs will be focused on this aspect of your Hill tenure, but many will. When you're hired, an employer is getting more than you—he or she getting your network, the threads that spread throughout the Hill and throughout other industries, with you in the center.

The network you build while on the Hill will last a lifetime. It will serve you no matter where you go or what you become. But it won't survive unless you give it constant attention. The hello email (or, better yet, call), the help you offer, and the support you give. These aren't Facebook friendships; they are true relationships and they will be your biggest advantage in life.

Tip #2: Character Counts

Remember the applicant nearly hired at Jaime's firm? (See page 137.) The person didn't get the job after Jaime made a few calls to the Hill to check in with those who had worked with the applicant. The short version is that the individual was not a great colleague and sometimes was a bully. We hope this applicant eventually found the right job; we hope even more this person changed their ways. As we said in chapter 9, your reputation is the most important thing you own while a staffer. The chances that someone you are about to meet has already checked up on you are high. This is true whether you're going to interview off the Hill or are meeting someone new on the Hill.

We've said it often enough: The kid fetching your coffee today might be your boss tomorrow. This is the way it works on the Hill. You never forget moments when you're made to feel small and insignificant. How likely is it that you'd stick your neck out for this person if you found yourself able to do so? And what would you say if someone called asking about this person—about how the person is to work with? Maybe you wouldn't be completely honest about how you felt, but you aren't going to be effusive with praise.

You don't want to be the one that the interns remember as a jerk. Some of those interns are going to be powerful people one day—and they will remember if you treated them like garbage. They might be able to help you get a job (or hire you themselves). Perhaps you were having bad day. If so, you should apologize the next day. It's incredibly difficult to get people to change their opinion of you after one bad encounter. But never think for a moment that they forgot. They didn't forget.

People respect talent and skills, but they respect character more. The best part is that character is the easiest one to master. Treat others with kindness and respect, no matter where they fall on the hierarchy. It's that easy. If you build a reputation as a person of character, as someone who is fair and kind, the doors off the Hill will swing open for you. You will be a person others want to help. You will be someone whom others think of when an opportunity falls into their lap. And you will find that everyone wants you on their team.

Tip #3: The Skills Advantage

The last piece of advice is short but important. Earlier we mentioned the path you will choose when you start your climb: policy or communications. You must choose one early in your career, because it's terribly difficult to shift course once you're on a path. The exception, as we mentioned, is if you work at the state or local level, because staffs are usually smaller, and everyone needs to be a jack-of-all-trades. The path you choose will also determine your choices when you decide to leave the Hill. What those choices are will be self-evident when the time comes, so there's no need to go into them here. Just know that the chances of being hired to analyze policy if you were a press secretary or conduct a press conference if you were a legislative assistant are slim.

When it comes to your skill set, there's another consideration. As a staffer, you will be introduced to cutting-edge tactics and technology. Politics is a fast-paced, competitive field, and new approaches and methods are attempted all the time. It's your job to learn these new ways: a new technology for analyzing data, a new medium for spreading information, or a new policy for bringing about change. You must always be on the lookout for opportunities to advance your skills.

You should also try to master these new ways. Become an expert in your chosen field. An expert isn't only good at the old methods; he or she is aware of the new ones as well. When Amos was put in charge of the brand-new digital domain for Representative Blunt, he had to become steeped in that brave new technology world. He had to know what was possible and how to implement it in the office. The point isn't that this allowed him to be better at his job and gave his member a competitive advantage, although both were certainly true. The point is that when Amos was ready to leave the Hill, he knew he could bring his digital expertise with him. He recognized a need off the Hill for someone with his skill set.

In other words, it's incumbent upon you to go beyond what's expected of you in your chosen path. You must constantly monitor what is being done in your field so you can become an expert. If you're in policy, that means reading the latest journals, not just what's on Twitter. If you're in communications, that means watching out for the new tech, not just following what everyone else is doing. Yes, this will take up your off-work hours, but that's part of expanding your skill set.

There is a misconception that the public sector is slower than the private sector. For bureaucracy and agencies, that's probably true. However, it's very much false for political organizations, such as Hill offices or campaign committees, which are caught in fierce competition. These are ideal places to advance your skills so that eventually you can bring your expertise to the private sector. You must make the most of your time. If you do, you can add value wherever you go.

WHERE WE WENT (AND HOW WE FELT)

You're probably wondering where we went after the Hill. Let's start with Amos. In December 2007, Amos had been working as press secretary for House Republican Whip Roy Blunt for nearly two years when he and his wife, Whitney, decided to start a family. Since he was in communications, Amos gravitated toward public relations, where he could put the things he had learned as a Hill pioneer in the digital space to good work. He soon found an opportunity at a DC-based firm as an assistant vice president. The job gave Amos and Whitney exactly what they wanted—a six-figure salary and the ability to start a family and continue living in Washington.

Amos hated leaving the Hill. He would come home from work and pester Whitney for information—for her part, the last thing she wanted to do was regurgitate the day's happenings. She wanted to relax. Amos would watch the news and miss the thrill of knowing that the featured stories were part of his efforts. Now he was on the other side; he was back to all but begging reporters to take his call. That's the trade-off. But Amos had another poker in the fire—an idea that was only starting to take shape. We'll return to that in the next chapter.

Exactly a year later, Jaime was finishing up his duties as floor director and counsel for House Democratic Whip James Clyburn. He had considered putting his law degree to use at a corporate law firm. Yes, the salary was nice—really nice—but Jaime felt going to a law firm would be a step back. As part of the whip operation, Jaime had corralled some of the most powerful members in Congress to vote for legislative measures. He was accustomed to being in command of his own operation, even if he was subordinate to Clyburn. But Clyburn trusted Jaime, and that gave him the power to act as he saw fit. At a firm, Jaime would have to start as an associate. He wouldn't be given his own cases and clients until he had put in a few years.

Instead, drawing on his political and policy knowledge, Jaime pursued a job in government relations and lobbying. His job-search efforts brought him to the attention of the Podesta Group. It seemed like the perfect fit. Jaime could expect a salary commensurate with his financial obligations, and he would remain intimately connected to the Hill, drawing on his understanding of Congress to help his clients. For now, he was content to start his new life. During his last few weeks on the Hill, Jaime met his future wife, Marie Boyd. What's more, the job gave Jaime the freedom to pursue other interests, such as doing political commentary and analysis for national television shows. He was learning how to express his ideas—*his* ideas—to a broader audience, an opportunity not afforded to staffers. Still, Jaime missed the Hill, and he felt that he wasn't quite done with it yet.

We found our new careers by using the tips in this chapter. It's not rocket science, but it does require some work and determination. Even Jaime, the old Hill hand, thinks he could have cut his six-month job search down a bit if he had tapped his network a bit more. That's why we've written this book—so you can learn from our mistakes. Know this: Having built a career on the Hill, you will always be a part of it. No matter where your future endeavors take you, you will never forget the experiences you had and the friendships you formed. They are what makes the Hill such a special place to work. Take them with you.

How They Climbed the Hill
JOSH SHULTZ'S STORY

My first experience with politics was an intern for House Majority Whip Tom DeLay. I had just finished my freshman year at Texas A&M, where I studied journalism. But my summer in Washington, DC, changed me. I fell in love with the town, its people, and especially the political world that had Capitol Hill at its center. After graduation, I was hired by DeLay as a staff assistant, before moving into the press shop. It was here, right when the internet was still in its infancy, that I forged my new role.

You must remember that at this time, in the early 2000s, many members didn't even have a website. The value of the internet as a medium for effective communication had not yet been realized in politics. Quite quickly, I found myself as the point person on new media—not so much because I was an expert but because everyone else was too busy. Being in leadership, DeLay had more interaction with the press than other members. He was also the kind of politician reporters loved—rough around the edges and always good for a sound bite. But why wait for the press to send out our message? I didn't know much about the digital world, but I knew we could bypass the traditional media with our own emails.

I started small, building a website using an early software known as FrontPage, and compiling press reports and clippings, which we blasted out to other members in the caucus. Rather than sending press releases to reporters only, we sent them to everyone we could. I carried this new focus on digital communications to the district office in Texas, encouraging the team there to take photos of DeLay with constituents and while he was out and about in the district. We put those on the website—a kind of precursor to Facebook and Instagram.

In 2007, I moved over to the National Republican Congressional Committee (NRCC) to head up its new media operations. By this point, I was well versed in digital and looked on in dismay at the unfortunate state of my new employer's digital landscape. All the departments were isolated from each other, with very little coordination between them. For instance, communications would send out a press release without informing the other departments, such as political or fund-raising. My job as director of new media was to tear down these silos and get the divisions talking to each other.

The other major aspect of my job in those days was to leverage the bloggers, whose numbers had exploded. Everyone seemingly had a blog. But just like inside the NRCC, the bloggers (on our side at least) were without any central direction or coordination. Although it was a bit like herding cats, I made a point of reaching out to the bloggers to get them pulling in the same direction. If we had an important race, I wanted as many bloggers as I could get covering it. I did this in a number of ways: we fed them information; we gave them access to candidates; and we featured them on our site and through our other channels.

It seems rather basic today, but at the time we were making it up as went along. That was the great joy of working at the NRCC: The competitive pressure forced us to experiment. We had this shiny brand-new toy called the internet, and no one was quite sure how to use it. So we innovated. Some things worked, but a lot didn't. To pull one example, I had assumed that working at the NRCC would put me in touch with the people running the campaigns on the ground. But that was the one silo I couldn't quite crack to my satisfaction. We should have focused more energy and resources on using the various digital channels to deliver the right information to the campaigns and to receive information from the campaigns in turn.

Nevertheless, the digital tools and expertise that I developed and honed, both on the Hill and at the NRCC, proved invaluable to my later career. Amos will tell you about our little venture called FamousDC.com. Today I run my own agency that specializes in Web development, multimedia production, and online communications. If it sounds very similar to what I started out doing in DeLay's office fifteen years ago, that's because it is.

—**JOSH SHULTZ,** president, NJI Media, and cofounder, FamousDC.com

CHAPTER 9

THE BEST LEADERSHIP COURSE IN THE WORLD

You read a book like this one expecting a reward. You read ours assuming that the reward is learning how to start and build a career in politics, whether in Washington or closer to home. That's certainly the main reward we offer, but this chapter is about the other reward—one that we can't give you, but which you will acquire as part of your government career. We'll say it as simply as we can: We wouldn't be the leaders we are today if not for our years as Hill staffers. Amos wouldn't have dreamed of starting his own public relations firm in his midthirties, and Jaime would never have been the associate chairman of the Democratic National Committee or chairman of the South Carolina Democratic Party. Likewise, our old colleagues whose stories you have read in this book have all reached the highest levels of their industries. They are presidents, vice presidents, founders, directors, and chiefs of staff. Their success (and ours) isn't a coincidence.

The Hill breeds success by building leaders and visionaries, and sending them out into the world. It doesn't consciously do this nor is that its purpose—you won't enter any "leadership training" seminar while a staffer. Rather, leadership and the ability to think big are the results of the quality and diversity of work one does on the Hill; the excellence and experience of one's mentors; and one's growing list of achievements. In other words, the Hill's leadership training is organic. It is a natural outcome of finding success as a staffer. Even if it is natural, you still must work for it.

For evidence, we offer our experience and the experience of our friends and colleagues. We can't find any surveys that track the career paths of former Hill staffers. We also can't think of anyone with whom we worked on the Hill who built a successful career on the Hill and then didn't go on to do great things afterward. Maybe not right away, but over the course of a career. You might leave the Hill because you are exhausted and need a change of pace. You might decide to pursue other ventures that offer more money and a better work-life balance. But the job you get immediately after the Hill isn't the metric we're using to talk about leadership. Our metric is more about the journey from the Hill to the next peak and the peak after that, each one progressively taller and grander.

The true reward of building a career as a staffer is long-lasting, meaningful success based on your leadership abilities. We cannot promise you a job on the Hill or in a state legislature, even if you do follow our advice in this book. But your chances may be much higher than the applicant who didn't read our book. However, we *can* promise that if you build a successful Hill career, you may be an outstanding leader whose abilities will match your ambitions—and those ambitions will be far larger and more realistic than you could ever have imagined as a newly minted staff assistant answering constituent phone calls.

How does the Hill do this? What should you expect?

FROM FAMOUS AMOS FIREWORKS TO FAMOUSDC.COM

Perhaps you recall that Amos helped run his family's fireworks store in Alabama, called Famous Amos Fireworks. We told you how managing a store, particularly on the customer service end, taught Amos the power of friendly chatter. We also told you how Amos utilized that skill on the Hill to start and grow his career. It turns out that wasn't the end of Famous Amos Fireworks's influence on its namesake. While Amos has remained firmly in communications since leaving the Hill, his career has taken several twists and turns. The one constant since leaving has been FamousDC.com, a site that owes its name to Famous Amos Fireworks, which kept Georgians and Alabamians stocked with explosives to celebrate the Fourth of July properly.

When Amos worked for Republican Whip Roy Blunt, he had a coveted floor pass, which allowed him to walk the floor of the House of Representatives. It was a special privilege, one that Amos knew he would greatly miss when he left the Hill at the end of 2007. With a floor pass, you are a witness to history being made. During one of his last weeks on the Hill, Amos strolled down to the floor to watch his final vote. He had no reason for being there, other than wanting to soak up as much as he could before he left. It was a sentimental moment, pure and simple. But that's the thing about the Hill; you never know when a simple walk will turn into a life-changing opportunity.

A few weeks earlier, Amos had had an idea. He didn't like the prospect of being on the "out" of politics, which is where he would be the moment he turned in his Hill badge. It wasn't so much the power and influence he knew he would miss as the Hill itself, the community. Think of a retiring athlete. He or she is going to miss the action, but they are going to miss teammates more—the spirit and sense of camaraderie that make a team game so special. The question kept Amos up a night: how can he stay connected to his old team?

The answer became Amos's idea. It would turn out to be a Big Idea, but Amos didn't know that at the time.

As he walked onto the House floor, Amos was approached by a staffer for House Minority Leader John Boehner, who asked him what he was up to. Amos replied that he was leaving the Hill, and this was his final floor vote. The Boehner staffer understood immediately. The staffer then asked Amos about his post-Hill plans. Amos replied that he was thinking about starting a website—a blog—that focused on

Hill staffers. A lot of sites covered Capitol Hill for the insider as well as the outsider. However, all these sites were (more or less) outlets that catered to readers interested in the news of the Hill. Some offered straight news; others focused on gossip, scandal, and political machinations. Amos wasn't interested in any of that, and not only because he had no desire to "report on" his one-time fellows. Let the journalists do that. No, Amos wanted to create a blog written *by* former and current Hill staffers *for* Hill staffers. Nothing like that existed, but Amos recognized a need and understood the digital tools to make it happen.

The staffer was intrigued and told Amos that he knew a bit about website design. Did Amos need some help? Yes, Amos most certainly did. A few days later, the staffer had emailed Amos some layouts for the new site. By the time Amos officially left Capitol Hill, his website was up and running . . . with one twist. It was anonymous. Aside from a few people, no one knew who was behind it.

A decade later, with a monthly reach of 3.2 million visits, FamousDC.com has an email subscription base of 20,000 readers. With his business partner Josh Shultz, Amos took his otherwise simple idea of staying attached to the Hill and turned it into a money-making venture, a must-read for anyone connected to the Hill community. Truthfully, Amos and Josh never imagined it would get so big or become so relevant to those working on the Hill. After all, the motive behind FamousDC.com was entirely self-serving. Amos wanted to stay in the loop.

Some ideas are meant to outgrow their origins. So it was with FamousDC.com. But these things don't just happen. A lot of good ideas catch fire, only to flame out as quickly. Once Amos and Josh recognized the demand, they utilized the tools and leadership skills they had each acquired working in politics to build FamousDC.com into a company. (Eventually they had to drop their anonymity.) That wasn't the plan, at least when Amos explained it on the House floor that day, but Amos didn't leave the Hill with the intention of doing small things. We doubt you will either.

We share Amos's story because it nicely captures how the Hill fosters leadership qualities in its veterans. First, there's the technical aspect. Amos was fortunate to work on the Hill during a period of digital upheaval. To help his boss, Amos had to come to grips with the new digital landscape, which was swiftly eclipsing the communications world that had dominated politics. Blogs, social media, the rapid decline of newspapers—these were the trends that Amos had to understand and know how to exploit to benefit his member. By learning about them, Amos became a digital communications expert. As an expert, Amos stood out among his peers. Here was a guy who knew how to work the new media channels to expand a message's reach. All the while, Amos was absorbing larger lessons and trends. He saw how digital communications could transform the private sector, which, as we said in the last chapter, isn't always more advanced than the public sector. He saw demand everywhere for the type of skills and digital tools he had acquired working in politics. One result was FamousDC.com.

The other result was that Amos became comfortable with execution. Ah, there's the big rub with leadership. Lots of people have lots of great ideas. But a great gaping chasm exists between an idea and execution—the ability to see that idea become reality. To get results. Yet the Hill, for all its obstruction and failed initiatives, is a place that prizes execution above all else. Votes, bills, alliances, story placement, endorsements—each requires a tremendous amount of skill to execute. You rise if you execute, or fall if you don't. Amos didn't only have an idea for a website focused on the Hill community. He knew that an idea is *never* enough. He had the confidence, courage, and skills to see that idea into action. The results speak for themselves.

Entrepreneurship is one channel where the leadership skills you acquire on the Hill can find purchase off the Hill. But there are so many more. Management, creativity, innovation—whatever your calling, you will have the courage and conviction that the skills you learned on the Hill will be sufficient to carry—to lead—your idea toward reality.

As for Jaime . . . he's going to let Amos have this little moment in the sun. We'll just say that in 2016 Jaime ran for chairman of the Democratic National Committee and is now the associate chair and counselor. FamousDC.com is a nice little website, though.

OUR THREE LEADERSHIP LESSONS

We don't want to give the impression that leadership simply happens on the Hill. You won't become an outstanding leader through osmosis. A lot depends on the type of person you are and what you want to accomplish. You probably don't know yet. As we said before, you will grow on the Hill, and your career ambitions will grow accordingly. Even if you aren't the type of person who wants to oversee others, the leadership skills that the Hill offers will certainly benefit you in whatever career you choose after politics. Remember, people who execute, who get results, are rare. They are highly sought after precisely because organizations know how rare they are.

With that in mind, we offer our three leadership lessons. Before we begin, we want to put them into context, since they explain how Jaime became the political leader he is today. Being a politician is an obvious career path for any former staffer. We debated whether to address how one becomes a politician, given Jaime's career, only to decide against it. Building a political career (as opposed to a career in politics) is a wholly different beast, and to do it justice, we would have to extend this book well beyond its scope and audience. That said, the following lessons, while intended for a career in any field, can be seen as the building blocks of a political career.

Leadership Lesson #1: Find Your Mentor

Some would-be politicians come to their ambition late in life. They've succeeded in their chosen professions, and only then do they decide to enter the arena. Not Jaime. It's hard to say if Jaime knew he wanted to be a politician the night he watched the Reverend Jesse Jackson speak at the Democratic National Convention in 1988—the night his grandfather let him stay up late.

Jaime does know that by the time he had begun working for Representative Clyburn, he wanted to do what Clyburn did. When he left the Hill, returning to the arena was always Jaime's plan. He recalls a conversation he had with Clyburn when trying to figure out what sort of job to take after the Hill. Clyburn knew Jaime's ambitions, and he supported them. So, it might sound strange that Clyburn advised Jaime to join the private sector first.

Why shouldn't Jaime start building his political base instead? Maybe run for the state legislature in South Carolina first?

Because, said Clyburn, Jaime had an advantage that African American politicians before him, officials from Clyburn's generation, didn't have. Clyburn mentioned that Black politicians of his era chose politics out of necessity. The private sector was mostly closed to them, insofar as it was a path to advancement and security. But the world had changed, and Jaime could ease his path toward politics by securing his financial situation at home first—paying off credit cards and student loans and taking care of his family. Then Jaime could launch his political career. He heeded his mentor's advice and joined a public relations and lobbying firm.

Clyburn's advice was of the kind that Jaime had come to expect from his longtime mentor. The wisdom behind it is that it advised patience—something most young people can't comprehend. When Jaime looks on the life he and his wife have built for their growing family, he knows that Clyburn advised him well.

This is one example out of dozens we could cite that reinforce the importance of having a mentor. Clyburn wasn't Jaime's only mentor during his Hill years. One other was Yelberton "Yebbie" Watkins, Clyburn's chief of staff. Except for Clyburn, no one had a greater influence on Jaime's growth as a Hill staffer (and person) than Yebbie. Yebbie taught Jaime the ins and outs of the Hill, even while he helped Jaime climb it. To this day, Jaime calls Yebbie and Clyburn to ask their advice on important decisions (and vice versa).

Much of this book is advice we learned from our mentors. But we can only give so much general advice. This is why a mentor is more than a civics teacher or career counselor. A real mentor helps guide the growth and maturity of you as a person. Maybe not consciously, but by watching and emulating your mentor, you will discover the secrets of success. We've done our best to list those secrets for you, but each person, every career, is different. You will discover your own success secrets as you rise. Most will come from the people you respect and admire. In time, you will impart these secrets to those who come after you.

The mentor relationship can be, but doesn't have to be, deliberate. In other words, you don't need to sit down for coffee with someone and ask that person to mentor you. (Chances are that individual has already decided to help you.) You also don't need to be coy about your intentions and expectations. The person you've chosen will understand what you are after, because they've been there before.

Our best advice on choosing the right mentor is to find the person in your office or another office whom you would want to be. In most cases, this person is one of your superiors, perhaps even the member. Use some sense when weighing your options. If it's your first day on the job (or first month), it's probably not the best idea to badger the member—or chief of staff, legislative director, or press secretary—to start teaching you. The member and staff don't know you, and they're not going to spend a lot of time (and trust) on you until they do. You must understand that of all the junior-level staffers working in an office at any one time, only a select few have any intention of staying long-term. No one wants to waste time on someone who's looking at the Hill as a good jumping-off point. So, give it time. Do your job. Your eagerness, willingness, and work ethic will be noticed.

Besides, mentors want protégés. Heck, we *wanted* to write this book because it serves the same purpose as mentorship. Given the absence of human resource departments in politics, no one is going to hand you the company guidebook to tell you what to do. The entire legislative operation is based on learning on the job. You can trace a line from the staffers today to the very first staffers of the First Continental

Congress, each new wave learning from the ones who came before. In other words, we know you need help and advice, and we want to give it.

Leadership Lesson #2: Find Common Ground

It's important to continually reach across the aisle and try to find common ground. After Jaime became chairman of the South Carolina Democratic Party in 2013, he made a point of reaching out to his counterpart on the Republican side, Matt Moore. Together, Jaime and Matt formed a working relationship, which turned into a friendship (see Matt's story in chapter 6). One collaboration that Jaime is particularly proud of is their efforts on prison reform in South Carolina. Matt and Jaime visited a local prison together and were able to build a bipartisan consensus on the need to overhaul how their state handled sentencing and incarceration based on new evidence that old ideas regarding crime were counterproductive.

This episode wasn't the first time Jaime learned the value of finding common ground to effect change. The lesson was drilled into him as a staffer on the Hill, from such titans as his friends Clyburn and Yebbie. Clyburn had great working relationships with members across the aisle, including golf buddy John Boehner, Representative Zach Wamp from Tennessee, and Representative Bud Shuster of Pennsylvania. The difference now is that it was Jaime's turn; he was the leader. It certainly helped that Jaime had such a willing and talented partner in Matt, who also understands the value of common ground.

In today's charged political environment, the idea of finding common ground seems impossible—even unsavory. At the same time, we complain that nothing ever gets done, at least in Washington. Maybe the two things are related? We're not going to try to solve the gridlock in American politics right now; instead, we want to smash the notion that you can't (and shouldn't) try working with the other side. The best leaders are those who can bring together competing interests to reach a shared objective. The idea that one should only do business with those who share your principles and interests isn't unrealistic; it's impossible. Some of our hardest moments on the Hill were trying to get our *own side* to agree to a certain objective. But that's how staffers learn the value of finding common ground. It is the *only* way to achieve results, no matter your industry.

Even in business, as a leader you will never have 100 percent buy-in from your team on an idea or initiative. If you do, you want to find better colleagues, since those who agree with you all the time aren't serving you very well. People aren't robots, and corralling a group of them to achieve an objective is difficult under any circumstance. The best leaders can manage the competing interests on their team and find the common ground. Moreover, true leaders can convince others to set aside their priorities to pursue the shared priority. Easier said than done, whether in business or in politics.

You will never truly appreciate how hard it is to get a bunch of people all pulling in the same direction until you work on the Hill. Frustrating doesn't begin to describe it. It can be maddening, soul-sucking, tedious work. Yet, occasionally, it happens and it's magical. Of course, it's not magic. It's the result of extremely talented leaders, who are experts of the art of finding common ground. Stick around the Hill long enough, and you will discover how it's done. When you're starting out, you will watch in awe as the masters of the Hill, members and staffers alike, achieve results. In time, you will have learned how to do it yourself. If you're good at it, we cannot overstate the value you can bring to any organization.

First, you must believe in the power of finding common ground. It's not a weakness; you're not "selling out" your side if you reach across the aisle. It all goes back to why you want to work in politics in the first place. As we said at the beginning, if your intent is to "crush" the other side, you will do poorly on the Hill. As a staffer in the legislative branch, your job is to help legislate. Leave the "crushing" to the party folks. Besides, there will never be a moment during your years as a staffer when your side can pass whatever it wants, however it wants. Even if your party controls both chambers and the White House, the need for common ground never disappears.

Remember, if your party is in the majority today, it might not be tomorrow. How you approach and treat the other side won't be forgotten when circumstances are reversed. Politics is a pendulum, and things are never as good or as bad as they appear. The real leaders on the other side will remember when you reached out to accomplish a shared goal. If they are now in the majority, the onus of getting results is on them—and they can't do that without you. To seek common ground is not only the best way to get results, it's an investment on future earnings.

Being able to find common ground is more complex than finding an issue everyone can agree on. It's more about understanding the motivations and underlying interests of your team—and the other side's team—and using them to your advantage. It's very psychological. You must understand the people with whom you're trying to find common ground. This means seeing them as people, not caricatures. If you believe what your allies in the media say about the other side, you will never accomplish anything. How could you? They're vicious monsters! They want to destroy the country! Who could work with such people?

You don't have to accept the principles of those on the other side to work with them, but you do have to see them as human beings. And treat them as human beings. The best leaders know how to do this, because politics (or business) is an industry in which theories collapse beneath the weight of human emotions and behavior. The Hill is the best place to learn about both, and how they work in tandem when someone makes a decision.

Leadership Lesson #3: Find Your First Principles

Working in politics, you will soon learn that the right ideas don't make someone a leader. You will see many bad leaders—elected officials or high-ranking staffers who say all the right things but couldn't lead a kid to a candy store. That's because ideology and correct beliefs have very little to do with leadership, particularly in government.

Ideology and beliefs are cheap; principles are expensive. And every good leader has a set of principles that guides his or her actions and conduct. If you've read this far, you can easily guess the kind of principles valued on the Hill. They don't only help you advance up the Hill; they will also serve you as a leader. The temptation to cut corners, to lash out at subordinates, to turn into a jerk is constant. The only reason people follow a jerk is because they're afraid to get fired. That's not how you motivate people. No one looks up to a jerk and says, "I'll follow him to the Gates of Hell!" The way you motivate people is by setting an example, by being someone worth emulating.

Principles inspire people, and inspiration is a critical component of leadership. On the Hill, you'll be surprised at how so few people have succumbed to cynicism. It's understandable when it happens, because the back-and-forth of politics can be a tedious experience. Which is why inspiring leaders are so important to the daily function of Hill life. Someone who can pick up the troops when morale is low is someone who can motivate a team to action. As a staffer, you will need to find your strength and determination almost daily. A great leader in the office makes it a lot easier.

How does the Hill help you find the principles that will guide you? By revealing that all the wrong principles don't help achieve results. The principles you hold most dear are the ones that you discovered during the tough moments. And on the Hill, you'll have plenty of those. But you will see how those above you rally and overcome the hard times; you'll also see that those with the wrong principles, or no principles at all, fail and often fall. Slowly, you will gather about you a set of principles critical to your success as a staffer. Not only are these the principles that help you navigate challenging moments, but they are also the ones you rely on to help influence others. If no one wants to follow a jerk, neither do they want to do a jerk's bidding. If you're attempting to work across the aisle, those on the other side want to know if you're a person who does business fairly and ethically.

We each knew that the other was a fair, responsible, and principled person. We knew each other's reputations from the Hill, and we had worked together before writing this book. Because we respected each other—we shared similar principles despite our ideological differences—we were able to work toward something big, something inspiring, something like this book.

Find your principles, stick with them, and you will see how others respond. You will become a leader worth following.

How They Climbed the Hill
TONYA WILLIAMS'S STORY

Like many who find their way into politics, my path was not linear. After graduating from law school (and a much-needed hiatus to travel around the world), I set out on a well-worn path to become a professional lawyer. Fortunately, it didn't take long to discover that practicing law was not my passion, which should not have been a surprise given the numerous hints and clues I casually ignored along the way. However, over the years I've learned that sometimes the only way to discover what you love is by doing things that you don't. In fact, for many people like me, Jaime, and Amos, who grow up in small towns with somewhat limited exposure, trial and error may be the only way.

Feeling a bit lost and a little scared about not knowing what I wanted to do professionally, I turned to colleagues, family, and friends for advice. With few exceptions, I was encouraged to pursue work in politics and policy. Within months, I landed a job in the office of Senator Marc Basnight, president pro tempore of the North Carolina Senate. Two months later, I was promoted to general counsel—that's how fast things can move, particularly at the state level where staff and resources are limited, but the opportunities to learn and influence are vast. I worked for Senator

Basnight for five incredible years, but learned one of the most valuable lessons during my first week on the job when my new boss came into my office and repeatedly asked me to sit down and stand up. After a few rounds of this seemingly ridiculous exercise, the Senator, who was quite amused, implored me to remember the difference between my butt and the seat. He cautioned that the true power was in the seats we were all honored to temporarily occupy, and he encouraged me to do as much good as I could while I held that seat. Throughout my career, I've never forgotten the Senator's words and have worked hard to use the power and privilege in my various roles to advance the work and positions I believe in.

Since securing my first job in politics, I have had the good fortune to work as an executive for a multinational corporation; the chief of staff for Representative G. K. Butterfield; the director of legislative affairs for Vice President Joe Biden at the White House; and the vice president for policy and communications at one of the largest philanthropic foundations in the country. But by far, my time on the Hill has been the most rewarding. While on the Hill, I worked in the majority and the minority; I whipped votes on the floor of the House and the Senate; I worked as a liaison between the executive and legislative branches of government; I met with CEOs, foreign leaders, celebrities, royalty, and even the pope; and I sat at numerous negotiating tables alongside my colleagues, both Republicans and Democrats, working to advance consequential foreign and domestic policy. During my time, I experienced incredible successes and a few humbling defeats, and it was the best work of my life—equal parts exciting and exhausting.

While every former staffer has his or her unique experience, one thing is universal: The people you meet, the relationships you form, and the lessons you learn as you go about your daily work on the Hill, whether mundane or monumental, will serve you well no matter where you go, or what you do. I could go on for pages and pages about the lessons I learned that have proved to be invaluable in my personal and professional life, but for the sake a brevity, here are just a few.

I learned that people are not their politics, and if you are going to be successful, you must approach everyone with respect and try to understand what they truly believe and why. I learned that relationships matter and that your first interaction with an ally or an opponent should never be accompanied by an "ask." I learned that you should never put people in a position where they can't say yes, that there is always a long game and a short game, and that understanding which you are playing is critical. I learned that no matter where you sit, or how much power and authority you have (or think you have), the only thing you really have at the end of the day is your word. I learned the importance of listening—as President Lyndon Johnson famously said, "You aren't learning anything when you're talking." I learned that you must thoroughly understand both sides of an argument to be an effective advocate or critic. I learned that diversity in decision making (racial, ethnic, gender, religious, and so on) is vital to authentic and long-lasting problem solving. I learned that experience and a solid reference almost always trump a prestigious education and advanced degrees. And I learned that there are few places in the world where a person of any age or persuasion, regardless of role or tenure, can work and be constantly challenged and exposed to as much information, access, and opportunity as you are when you work at the US Capitol.

—TONYA WILLIAMS, former director of legislative affairs for Vice President Biden

#DOBIGTHINGS

The Hill will train you how to be a leader. Stay long enough and rise high enough, and you will learn what it takes to get things done. You will learn how to build a team and push that team toward a common goal and achieve it. Perhaps most important of all, you will want to. The Hill will give you the confidence and the courage to believe that you can do Big Things.

On his social media channels, Amos likes to promote his friends and colleagues who are engaged in big, meaningful projects. He adds the hashtag #DoBigThings at the end of each post. It's like a personal motto, and we want it to be your motto too. You've taken the first step toward doing Big Things by wanting to work in politics. But you've only started your journey. Neither of us could have imagined where we'd end up when we looked up at the Capitol dome with youthful eyes full of idealism. Nor did most of those whose stories you have read in these pages. We all started at the same spot, and yet we've all gone on to accomplish remarkable things in a variety of fields. The one commonality, other than our shared experience on the Hill, is that we've all turned into leaders.

You will, too. You must, if you hope to achieve Big Things in your career. The desire to make a difference doesn't end when you step off the Hill. In many ways, that's when it truly begins. When you're ready to leave the Hill, you'll be armed with the experience, the skills, and the conviction that you can make a difference. You will have seen cutting new technology, vibrant, bold ideas, and the remarkable effort it takes to achieve nearly impossible goals. You will see opportunities. These experiences will inspire you; they will make you want to take what you have learned and forge your own success.

Climb the Hill and you will be ready to conquer the mountains beyond.

A SERVANT OF THE FLAME

In June 1791, after many months surveying the site of the future capital city, Pierre Charles L'Enfant wrote President George Washington the following:

> After much menutial [sic] search for an eligible situation ... I could discover no one so advantageously to greet the congressional building as is that on the west end of Jenkins heights, which stand as a pedestal waiting for a monument. ... Some might, perhaps, require less labor to be made agreeable, but, after all assistance of arts, none ever would be made so grand.

L'Enfant's vision for his "pedestal" was spot-on. Today, atop what he called Jenkins Heights is indeed a grand monument, the US Capitol Building. Like all good history, the story is not without interesting side notes. Up until L'Enfant's letters, there never had been a place called Jenkins Heights (or Hill), certainly not at that location. The hill that dominated the marshy countryside was owned by one Daniel Carroll and known to the local landowners as "New Troy"—a far more fitting name for the future Capitol Hill.

After all, the Founding Fathers viewed their bold experiment in a democratic republic as heir to a classical tradition stretching back to ancient Athens and the Roman Republic, with its elected representatives, senate, and popular assemblies. The comparison extended beyond ideas and institutions. For laying down his command and "returning to his fields," George Washington was compared to the mythic Cincinnatus—a Roman farmer called upon to save the republic from its enemies before giving up his dictatorial powers.

That L'Enfant chose to place the seat of this new republic on a hill known as New Troy is coincidence, but a darn good one. In Virgil's *Aeneid,* the proto-Roman hero Aeneas escapes from the destruction of Troy at the hands of the conquering Greeks and founds a New Troy—Rome—on the Italian peninsula, beside the Tiber River. It's also a coincidence that one of Daniel Carroll's neighbors, Francis Pope, who lived on the other side of a small stream that extended from the Potomac River, called his farm Rome and the creek Tiber. (Its dull, original name was Goose Creek.)

Sadly, it would be L'Enfant's label, not Carroll's, that history would remember. Most guidebooks use Jenkins Heights or Hill even today. The strange part is that no one is quite sure where L'Enfant got the name in the first place. As one historian from the early twentieth century wrote: "The exact reason that the name Jenkins is continually associated with this hallowed spot remains to be explained." Not much has changed. In the end, we like to think it's one more "gift" that L'Enfant, the original designer of this great, confusing city, left for DC residents.

Of course, solving the mystery of Jenkins Heights is not why we wrote this book. While it's always a good thing to know a little something about your future office building, if only to show off to your boss at the interview, this bit of trivia won't help you build a career in Congress. But we believe it does put some things about working on Capitol Hill in the proper context, which will be very useful to you.

Rarely have the citizens of a state had the ability to help chart the course of their nation—and, in the case of the United States, the world. Those moments when it has occurred have been like a shooting star—a brilliant flash across a sky black with tyrants and despots that disappears in an instant. America's Founding Fathers understood this implicitly, which is one reason they were so conscious of their connection to the great republics of the past—the Greeks, the Romans, and, despite a recent war, the British. They were equally as conscious of how swiftly those republics winked out, to be replaced, almost invariably, by autocrats or oligarchs.

You live in one of those moments. Our shooting star still blazes. We must continue pushing. We must continue challenging and being the best we can. One day our story may flame out, but not yet.

If you learn nothing else from us, we hope that you at least learn this: Every morning you will climb a hill atop which sits the seat of the most powerful government on Earth, a hill once wooded and nondescript, but which nevertheless had been known by the fateful name of New Troy. On you and the few thousand people who climb the hill with you rests the responsibility of history that asks one thing above all else—respect the opportunity granted to you and work today as though the star will flame out tomorrow. Climb that hill and make a difference!

EPILOGUE

We hope this book has given you the blueprint to build a career in politics, and a meaningful one at that—one in which you can make a difference. The point of all this is not to simply collect a paycheck every two weeks or to meet friends for drinks at an evening political reception; we climbed the Hill because we wanted to make a positive difference in the lives of everyday Americans. To drill down further on this idea, we will share one last story from Jaime's time as floor director.

In October 1998, the country was rocked by the brutal beating, torture, and eventual death of a twenty-one-year-old University of Wyoming student named Matthew Shepard. His assailants were convicted of murder, and many believe his murder was motivated by his sexual orientation. As a result of Matthew's death, people began calling for legislation that would extend federal hate crimes prosecution to violent crimes committed on the basis of sexual orientation. After Democrats won the majority in both chambers of Congress in 2006, hate crimes legislation advocates had renewed faith that such a bill could finally pass.

On March 30, 2007, Congressman John Conyers, chairman of the House Judiciary Committee sponsored H.R. 1592, the Hate Crimes Prevention Act. At the time, current law only defined hate crimes as acts of violence motivated by race, religion, color, or national origin. The bill extended hate crimes protections to those who were victims because of their gender, sexual orientation, gender identity, or disability. The expansion of hate crimes to include these new categories was seen as controversial, and opponents argued that state and local laws already covered the crimes it addressed, therefore there was no need for federal involvement. President George W. Bush even threatened to veto any such legislation that was sent to him.

Nonetheless, Speaker Nancy Pelosi and many members of the House Democratic Caucus were committed to bringing this legislation to the house floor for a vote and passage. As we have learned, floor consideration meant the whip operation, and the whip operation meant Jaime. Speaker Pelosi gave Majority Whip James Clyburn and his whip operation led by Jaime less than a week to garner the support needed. On Monday, April 30, 2007, Jaime and his team began whipping the bill: They sent out a detailed summary of the bill, released a series of whip questions asking offices where they stood on the bill, and began gathering whip question responses from member offices.

Jaime quickly realized that this bill was not like others. Whereas members would normally either answer the whip question with "undecided" or choose not to respond immediately, this bill, so early in the process, had already garnered more than thirty "no" and "leaning no" votes—enough to kill passage of the bill. Clyburn, Jaime, and the whip team, concerned with the early opposition from some of the more conservative Democrats in the caucus, gathered the Democratic leadership to discuss the opposition and what could be done to pass the bill by Pelosi's May 3 deadline.

In an effort to garner support, Jaime and his team began to solicit the help of third-party organizations such as the Human Rights Campaign, Interfaith Alliance, and Leadership Conference on Civil Rights. In addition, the whip's office disseminated stories of crimes that were not covered by current law. One such story was that of Brandon Teena, targeted and killed because of gender identity. Teena, twenty-one, was raped by two friends after they discovered he was biologically female. After the rape and assault, Teena reported the crime to the police but the deputies were not allowed to arrest those responsible. Five days later, on New Year's Eve 1993, the two men found Teena. They shot and stabbed him to death.

It was stories like this and the efforts by Members of Congress like representatives Tammy Baldwin, Barney Frank, and John Lewis that helped to move some of the "no" votes to "yes," but by Wednesday morning it was not enough. The Democratic whip count was still at 195 "yes" votes, 23 votes away from the magical 216 votes needed for passage. There were about 24 Democratic members at "no" when House Democrats could only afford to lose 17 votes. Pelosi, Clyburn, and their teams were running out of time, and then it happened: Jaime can't recall whose idea it was, but it ended up being a master stroke. Pelosi and the Caucus decided to invite Matthew's mom, Judy, and one of the sheriffs from the Albany County Sheriff's Department to address the members of the House Democratic Caucus at the Thursday morning whip meeting.

The morning whip meeting began with Majority Whip Clyburn asking several members to speak, including representatives Barney Frank and John Lewis. They gave impassioned speeches about the importance of the bill and how it reflected the values of the Democratic Party and America. Speaker Pelosi then introduced Judy Shepard and the sheriff. Jaime had experienced some amazing political moments up to that one, but nothing like this particular instance. The sheriff discussed the importance of having these protections in law enforcement, and Judy humanized the bill and spoke about her son. She spoke about her hopes and dreams for him, and she spoke about the anguish and pain of losing him to those who hated him for who he was. As she spoke, there was not one dry eye in the room, and as luck would have it, several of the members who were listed as "no" or "leaning no" attended the meeting that morning. Afterward, some members told Jaime that they had imagined Matthew to be their son or daughter, and they thought about the pain they would have felt in that situation. House Democrats went into that morning meeting with 195 Democratic "yes" votes and by that afternoon the bill passed on the floor with a final vote of 237–180; ultimately

212 Democrats and 25 Republicans voted for final passage. (The biggest hurdle was the Motion to Recommit procedural vote that garnered 216 Democratic "yes" votes.) A similar bill was passed in the Senate, but the bill did not ultimately become a law until President Obama signed it in October 2009. Nonetheless, it was the efforts of so many, including Jaime, that ultimately helped to make the difference.

This story is a testament that we all can make a difference. *You* can make a difference! You can impact the lives of many, but first you need to take the initial steps to climbing the Hill!

RESOURCES

INTERNSHIPS AND FELLOWSHIPS

Asian Pacific American Institute for Congressional Studies (APAICS)

APAICS, a nonprofit organization associated with the Congressional Asian Pacific American Caucus, offers a year-long legislative and policy fellowship program for graduates and young professionals. Fellows receive a stipend, medical insurance, and airfare. To qualify for the fellowship, applicants must have completed their undergraduate degree, and be US citizens, lawful permanent residents, or individuals who are legally authorized to work full-time without restriction for any US employer. APAICS also has a summer and fall internship program. Interns receive stipends and airfare. Housing is not provided. To be eligible for the internship, applicants must be eighteen years of age at the start of the internship, a full-time undergraduate student currently enrolled or recently graduated, and a US citizen or legal permanent resident. Individuals under the Deferred Action for Childhood Arrival policy must possess an employment authorization document.
apaics.org

American Legion Boys State/Boys Nation and Girls State/Girls Nation

Boys State, sponsored by the American Legion, and Girls State, sponsored by the American Legion Auxiliary, are educational and leadership training programs for high school students. The goal of these programs is to give the students a better understanding of the structure and function of local, state, and federal government. Boys State and Girls State members participate in a nonpartisan curriculum that includes legislative sessions, assemblies, and other immersive learning experiences. To be eligible, students must have completed their junior year in high school and have at least one semester remaining. They also must be a legal inhabitant of the United States.

www.legion.org/boysnation/stateabout

www.alaforveterans.org/ALA-Girls-State/

College to Congress

College to Congress is a nonprofit organization that provides scholarships and leadership training for low-income college students seeking internships in Congress. To be eligible, applicants must be undergraduate students who qualify or receive Federal Pell Grants. College to Congress helps these college students secure hard-to-get congressional internships and covers all the costs associated with the summer internship including travel, housing, meals, and even professional wardrobe. For some of these young interns, it's the first time they've ever worn a suit or professional attire. The program matches interns with experienced Hill staffers from the opposite party to build bipartisan relationships. These relationships are key to breaking down the partisan divide that prevents our nation from finding a middle ground on legislative issues.

Without College to Congress, many of these students would never have a chance to intern on Capitol Hill because of their financial situation. By helping Congress fill these internships, College to Congress is building a more diverse and inclusive landscape on Capitol Hill, providing low-income students the chance to pursue careers in public service, and putting voices that represent the entire socioeconomic scale into the nation's leader's offices.

www.collegetocongress.org

Congressional Black Caucus Foundation (CBCF)

CBCF, a nonprofit organization associated with the African American members of Congress (Congressional Black Caucus), offers three fellowships: the Congressional Fellowship, the Congressional Fellowship on Women in Health Sciences Leadership, and the Donald M. Payne Foreign Policy Fellowship. Fellows receive an annual salary plus benefits. Fellowship applicants must be US citizens or have a permit to work in the United States for the duration of the program. In addition, they must have a graduate or professional degree completed prior to the fellowship start date. The CBCF also has a summer internship that provides housing and a stipend. Applicants must have a minimum GPA of 2.5 on a 4.0 scale; be at least a college sophomore at the time of application; and be a US citizen or have a permit to work in the United States. In addition, they are required to live or go to school in a Congressional Black Caucus member's district.
www.cbcfinc.org

Congressional Black Caucus Institute (CBCI)

CBCI, is a nonprofit organization associated with the African American members of Congress (Congressional Black Caucus). The CBCI offers a Political Leadership Development Program called the Boot Camp. The Boot Camp is offered every summer in Washington, DC, and participants are given an interactive crash course on political campaigns. To be eligible for the program, applicants must be US citizens who are registered to vote. Applications that are submitted by the deadline are given to a candidate's perspective member of Congress, and the member will determine who will be selected to attend the program. In most cases, members of Congress cover the total or a portion of the cost of participation, including lodging. Nonetheless it depends upon each individual member. Graduates of this program have gone on to an assortment of political jobs from being elected to office to serving as a party officer to running campaigns.
cbcinstitute.org

Congressional Hispanic Caucus Institute (CHCI)

CHCI is a nonprofit organization associated with the Hispanic and Latino members of Congress (Congressional Hispanic Caucus). The CHCI Public Policy Fellowship Program provides an annual salary, benefits, and airfare. To be eligible for the fellowship, applicants must have earned a bachelor's degree within two years of the program start date and have a 3.0 GPA or higher. They also must be US citizens, lawful permanent residents, asylees, or individuals who are lawfully authorized to work full-time without restriction for any US employer and who, at the time of application, possess lawful evidence of employment authorization. Individuals who are seeking consideration under the Deferred Action for Childhood Arrival policy must possess an employment authorization document at the time of application. Summer, fall, and spring internships provide transportation, housing, and a stipend. Applicants must currently be enrolled full-time and working toward their undergraduate degree. The internship program has the same academic and residency requirements of the fellowship program.

chci.org

Democratic National Committee (DNC) and Republican National Committee (RNC)

The DNC and the RNC, the national party committees, are ultimately responsible for the presidential primary nominating process and assisting in national and local elections. Each committee has summer, spring, and fall internships during which interns experience and learn more about national politics. Interns are assigned to various departments within the political organizations. The DNC and RNC require applicants to complete the internship application and submit a resume and letters of recommendations. Links to state parties can be found on these sites as well. State party committees also provide summer- and semester-long internship opportunities.

www.democrats.org

www.gop.com

National Conference of State Legislatures (NCSL)

A nonpartisan association representing state legislatures and their members, the NCSL provides a listing of internship and fellowship programs and their contacts in each state and US territory. Each state has a different program and application requirements.
www.ncsl.org

Running Start

This nonpartisan organization works to inspire and train the next generation of young women political leaders through a variety of programming. The Young Women's Political Leadership Program teaches high school girls about political leadership, and the Running Start/Walmart Star Fellowship Program does the same for college-age women. These fellows intern in the office of a female member of Congress and receive political leadership training. Fellows are provided free accommodations and a semester stipend. Applicants must be college-aged women who are juniors or seniors, or who are within one year of graduating from undergrad.
runningstartonline.org

United States Senate Youth Program (USSYP)

USSYP is a college scholarship and week-long educational leadership experience for outstanding high school students interested in public service careers. The program is sponsored by the US Senate and funded by the Hearst Foundations. Two high school juniors or seniors who hold elected office in their student government are selected every year from each state, the District of Columbia, and the Department of Defense. These 104 students serve as delegates and meet elected and appointed officials from the executive, legislative, and judicial branches of of government. Transportation, accommodations, and meals are provided. Students also receive a substantial college scholarship to the college or university of their choice. To qualify, students must hold student body office or another elected or appointed position in their communities, and show academic interest and aptitude in government, history, and politics. Selection processes vary by state, but many states administer a comprehensive public affairs, government, and history test prepared annually for the program by a college professor of political science. States may also ask for additional essays and/or personal interviews.

ussenateyouth.org

The Washington Center for Internships and Academic Seminars (TWC)

This independent nonprofit connects students with internship opportunities for academic credit. TWC runs two signature programs in addition to serving as an information hub for other intern and fellowship opportunities in Washington, DC. To be eligible to participate in this program, applicants must be at least eighteen years old; must be enrolled as an undergraduate student at an accredited college or university, must be a sophomore or above while participating in the program (and have completed at least two semesters on campus); must maintain a grade point average of at least 2.75 on a 4.0 scale; must be able to receive academic credit from their college or university for their participation; and must have approval from campus liaison or faculty sponsor.

www.twc.edu

Washington Intern Student Housing (WISH)

WISH provides affordable, furnished intern-only row house and apartment housing for students in Washington, DC.

internsdc.com

EMPLOYMENT SEARCH, PROFESSIONAL DEVELOPMENT, AND NETWORKING

Cloture Club

Started by two former congressional staffers, Cloture Club began as the exclusive events list for networking on or around Capitol Hill. This list helps staffers connect with political leaders and occasionally provides low-cost dining options. Founders of the website find ways to engage their audience through creative content surrounding the inner workings of Capitol Hill. Website articles such as "Muppets in Congress," "Tea Party Insult Generator," and the annual "State of the Union Drinking Game" have attracted national attention and have quickly become internet favorites.

www.clotureclub.com

FamousDC

FamousDC began as a hobby in 2007 and has grown into a digital media empire. Reaching over 3.2 million people per month, the online magazine has become the go-to resource for people, places, and things to do in the District of Columbia. Today, FamousDC's audience begins on Capitol Hill and expands across the country. FamousDC's mission is to bring out the best within its community from Capitol Hill staffers to K Street lobbyists and other highly regarded influencers. Through appearances on Fox News and by hosting 2016 Presidential Primary/Convention events in Las Vegas, Miami, Houston, and Boulder, FamousDC made its mark as a Washington, DC, networking conduit, bringing together Republican and Democratic members of Congress and news and entertainment celebrities like Shaquille O'Neal, Martha Raddatz, Bret Baier, Mark McGrath, and more.

www.famousdc.com

Inclusv

Inclusv is an organization pushing for greater racial diversity among staff, consultants, and vendors and is an important source of information about job opportunities, professional development training, and mentorships in the political arena for people of color. It hosts a talent of color resume bank/database and provides employers with culturally competent career development training for staff.
inclusv.com

Legistorm

Legistorm is a web-based tool and database that contains valuable contact and biographical information on congressional staff. This site can be used to research a variety of useful topics, such as congressional positions and salaries for congressional offices and committees. The site even tracks information such as congressional offices that pay staffs the highest/lowest salaries and the offices that have the highest staff turnover. The site hopes to expand its coverage to include state legislatures as well. Legistorm is an invaluable tool for those negotiating title and salary.
www.legistorm.com

LinkedIn

LinkedIn can be a useful networking and research tool for political networking and job searches. The key determinant to getting a job on Capitol Hill, and politics in general, is establishing a relationship or a tie with the person making the hiring decision. LinkedIn is one of the best tools in determining whether someone in your network (a friend or colleague) has an existing tie or relationship with the individual ultimately making the hiring decision. Use your LinkedIn contacts to network and establish introductions and relationships with others in the political arena. It is important to keep your profile up-to-date (and professional) with the latest contact and career information. Employers also use the site to research those applying for positions.
www.linkedin.com

National Association of Diverse Consultants (NADC)

NADC is the largest association of diverse political and public affairs professionals. Launched in 2017, the membership-based group consists of political consultants, pollsters, lobbyists, and campaign vendors. The association was created to build a publicly available network and database of consultants that include women, members of the LGBTQ community, and communities of color. Members participate in networking/training events and are provided information on employment opportunities, campaign-related requests for proposals, and more.
www.thenadc.com

Tom Manatos Jobs

Known as one of the premier jobs lists on Capitol Hill and in Washington, DC, Tom Manatos Jobs has helped thousands of people find government and political jobs since 2002. This site has become the go-to place to find information regarding Hill related jobs, fellowships, and internships.
www.tommanatosjobs.com

US House of Representatives

The House oversees the House Vacancy Announcement and Placement Service, which helps members of Congress and committees fill staff vacancies. HVAPS also maintains a bank of resumes kept on file for a ninety-day period. A jobs bulletin with available opportunities is issued every week.
www.house.gov/employment/positions-with-members-and-committees

US Senate

The Senate posts the Senate Employment Bulletin, which lists current jobs, internships, and positions that are available. It also maintains a resume bank to assist Senate offices and committees looking to fill vacancies.

www.senate.gov/visiting/employment.htm

The Victory Institute

The institute provides training and professional development programs for LGBTQ leaders who can further equality at all levels of government. Each year the Victory Institute assists hundreds of individuals who go on to influential careers in politics, government, business, and advocacy.

victoryinstitute.org

Other government job search sites:

USA Jobs: www.usajobs.gov

Roll Call Jobs: www.rcjobs.com

The Hill: thehill.com/resources/classifieds/employer

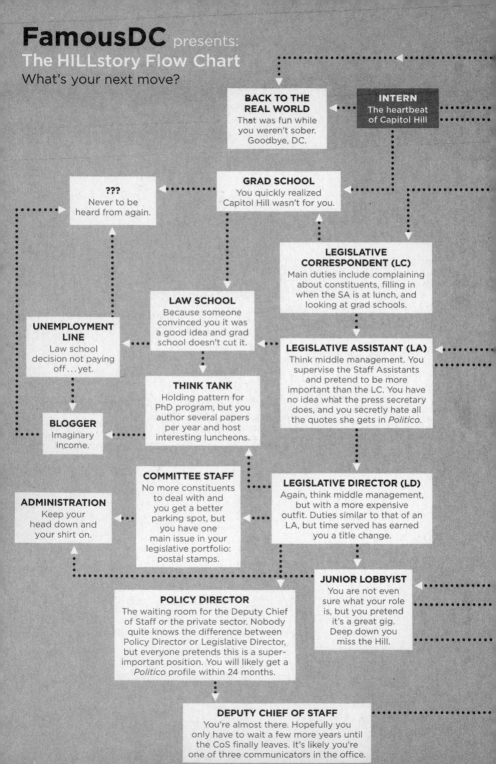

2ND INTERNSHIP
Because after the first internship, you still don't have a job.

SCHEDULER
Arguably the most important position on the staff, but the paycheck doesn't match up. Note: All requests must be made in writing.

STAFF ASSISTANT (SA)
Duties include phones, tours, mail, and scheduling happy hours. You're also in charge of softball field reservation.

PRESS ASSISTANT
A staff assistant with a better title. Officially in charge of press clips. The weekly conference communications meeting is your Super Bowl. The bartender at Tortilla Coast learns your first name.

PRESS SECRETARY
Using Facebook and Twitter is often your only press strategy. Responsible for media lists, pitch attempts, and always the first to happy hour.

DIGITAL COMMUNICATIONS DIRECTOR
Lord of the Tweets and master of Facebook. You're familiar with creative tools, just not great at using them. Amateur photographer. Everyone in the office thinks you can make things go viral.

COMMUNICATIONS DIRECTOR
Messaging guru. First line of defense when things hit the fan. First to complain when the policy shop doesn't respond quick enough. You spend hours at bars trying to explain the difference between you and the press secretary.

VP AT PUBLIC RELATIONS FIRM
Don't get too excited, everyone is a VP. Your day-to-day is mostly filled with writing columns and tweets for clients. You're occasionally allowed to flex the corporate card at BLT Steak.

SR. VP AT PUBLIC RELATIONS FIRM
The corporate card is all yours, and you're no longer writing blog posts; however, landing new business is hard. "You don't really lobby?"

CHIEF OF STAFF (CoS)
The job you've dreamed of since arriving on Capitol Hill. The only person the boss truly listens to when they find themselves knee-deep in a tough situation. Otherwise, you're just the person who refuses to let people leave early on Friday.

SENIOR LOBBYIST
Two years and 120 fund-raisers later, the new title is yours. Now the campaign committees want you to max out.

PARTNER
Whether it's PR, a law firm, or a lobbying group, everyone wants to be partner. Enjoy the golf course!

ACKNOWLEDGMENTS

AMOS SNEAD

First, I would like to thank my wife, Whitney Drew. You have been an amazing supporter of every crazy idea I have ever dreamed up. You are a wonderful mom to our kiddos and I am thankful we get to spend our lives keeping up with the Sneads!

To Emery, Harrison, and Barrett, I hope you read this book one day and each decide to follow a dream of your own. And remember, if you miss—try, try again.

Thank you to my family: my parents Brad and Ann Snead, my brothers Joel and Mark Snead. We started out selling fireworks on Highway 411 in Northeast Alabama and now I'm writing acknowledgments for a book about Congress. You each taught me to think big and end the show with a strong finale.

Thank you to all of the teachers along the way. I would like to especially thank Gary Davis of Cherokee County High School in Centre, Alabama, for first introducing me to creative writing.

To the S-3 family, let's keep building an empire. I consider it an honor to work alongside Rob Collins, Mike Ference, John Scofield, Tara Bauer, Matt Bravo, Noelle Clemente, Martin Delgado, Kate Dickens, Stephanie Genco, Lisa Kramer, Arjun Mody, Andrea Riccio, and Todd Wooten.

To the Alabama Army, thank you for starting the couch circuit and helping many people move from Alabama to Washington, DC. Thank you Jason Britt, Collier Craft, Aaron Latham, Alex Igou, Fred Miller, Leroy Nix, and Willie Phillips.

To the FamousDC team, supporters, and Friday Round-Up tipsters, thank you for making Washington, DC, and Capitol Hill a more interesting place to live, work, and play. Thank you Josh Shultz, Nathan Imperiale, Drew Ellis, Andrew Fimka, Natasha Flint, Marie Formica, Morgan Gress, Paige Gress, Ryan Hill, DJ Jamiel, Taz Jones, and Kathryn Lyons. We threw a party in Las Vegas with Ken Bone!

I also want to thank everyone I got to know and work with on Capitol Hill. From the fifth floor of Cannon HOB crew to the Blunt Force family (2006 and 2007 Congressional Co-Ed Football League Champions). There are way too many people to thank in this section. Capitol Hill is a place where many people work every day for something they believe in. Thank you all for helping shape our country.

To Blake Dvorak, you are a patient man! Thank you for keeping us on track, and thank you for believing in us—especially close to deadline.

To the great Shawn Pasternak, you are a gifted researcher and writer. Thank you for your quick analysis and research. I wish I could enter a smirk emoji here.

To Dana Newman, I still have the email you sent on July 5, 2017, telling us Ten Speed Press was interested in our book. Thank you for taking us over the finish line.

Thank you to the amazing team at Ten Speed Press: Lisa Westmoreland, acquiring editor; Emma Rudolph, editor; Michelle Li, Mari Gill, and Chloe Rawlins, designers; Dan Myers, production; Windy Dorresteyn, marketing strategist; and Kristin Casemore, publicist.

To my coauthor, Jaime Harrison, thank you for agreeing to speak—for no charge!—to that group of students visiting Washington for the first time from South Carolina. Your willingness to help others started a friendship that turned into a book. Keep doing big things!

JAIME HARRISON

Dum spiro spero. "While I breathe, I hope."

This book is for those fascinated by politics and its power to change people's lives. This book is for those who believe that the American Dream is not for a select few but can be enjoyed and experienced by all. This book is for those little boys and girls who grow up in impoverished communities devoid of hope and overflowing with low expectations. As the naysayers constantly tell them they can't, this book is their testament that they can and they will climb the Hill!

First, I want to thank my wonderful wife, Marie, and our son, William. The two of you have been my inspiration, and your love fuels me. Marie, I dedicate this book to you . . . thank you for being my best friend and my biggest fan. I love you!

I want to thank my entire family, particularly my parents Patricia and Rodney Stewart, my in-laws Harvey and Sherryl Boyd, my grandparents Jimmie Lou (Ms. Bookie) and Willie (Mr. Bookie) Harrison, and Ron and Patsy Stewart, siblings Ashley, Nate, and Dave (yeah, I included you, Drewesy), Robert, aunts, uncles, and cousins for their unwavering love and encouragement.

Thanks to my former teachers, classmates, friends, colleagues, and members of Congress who equipped me for every step of my journey. Thank you to my mentors: the late representative Earl Middleton, Senator John Matthews, Master Harvey Goldblatt, and J.B. Schramm.

Climbing the Hill would not have been worthwhile without my Clyburn Hill family. From our legendary holiday feasts to issuing "open invitations" on the House floor to hilarious Danny/Jennie/Barvetta/Lindy/Acacia/Andrea personal office debates, Clyburn staffers work very hard while having a lot of fun doing it. To my Clyburn Family (district, personal, leadership office colleagues (caucus/whip), and interns), thank you for always having my back! Also, a special shoutout to my Hill Rat Pack: Munir, Micah, Bernard, Sydney, Albert, Adam, Jon, Shawn, Dion, and David Robinson (RIP, brother, we miss you)!

I also want to thank my colleagues and friends at College Summit, Podesta Group, SC Democratic Party, Jaime for DNC Chair Team, and DNC. It was hard at times wearing multiple hats, and I wouldn't have been able to do it without your support. David (Kusnet), thanks for the title and guidance my friend!

To my political father, Congressman Jim Clyburn, you have taught me so much and have been my mentor, inspiration, and career guide post. Thank you and Ms. Emily for always believing in me and giving me an opportunity when others would not.

If Congressman Clyburn is my political father, then Yebbie Watkins and Clay Middleton are my political brothers. You each have taught me so much about friendship, loyalty, and humility. Thank you! Clay, outside of Marie, I don't think there has been anyone who has stayed on my case more about getting this book done! Love you, brother!

To Blake Dvorak, this book would not have happened without you! You are an amazing thought partner and a gifted writer. Thank you for helping us navigate this process. To Dana Newman, thank you! You are a class act and one hell of an agent!

To Elizabeth Morra, Anant Raut, Nadeam Elshami, Jon Samuels, Matt Moore, Tonya Williams, Eric Feldman, and Angela Rye: Thank you for your friendship and for agreeing to share your amazing stories or provide insight on how you successfully climbed the Hill.

A huge thank-you to our amazing team at Ten Speed Press: Lisa Westmoreland, acquiring editor; Emma Rudolph, editor; Michelle Li, Mari Gill, and Chloe Rawlins, designers; Dan Myers, production; Windy Dorresteyn, marketing strategist; and Kristin Casemore, publicist. Thank you for all of your efforts to make this dream a reality!

Finally, to my coauthor and friend, Amos Snead: Dude, this has been fun! Who would have thought two southern boys from Alabama and South Carolina would make it to DC and then write a book about succeeding on Capitol Hill?! I am so glad that you were my partner in this amazing journey! When do we begin the next book?!

ABOUT THE AUTHORS

AMOS SNEAD

Amos Snead is an innovator whose personable approach to communications is matched by his long list of accomplishments in the field. Snead is a founding Partner at S-3 Public Affairs, where he draws from in-depth experience working with leading print, television, and online journalists to counsel clients on digital communications and media strategies.

Prior to S-3 Public Affairs, Snead was a principal at a leading Washington, DC, public affairs firm, counseling Fortune 500 companies in the technology, energy, and healthcare industries, and serving as the primary spokesman for a range of high-profile clients.

Snead started his career on Capitol Hill, first as a press aide for the House Energy and Commerce Committee under Chairman Billy Tauzin (R-LA) and Chairman Joe Barton (R-TX), then as communications director for Congressman Louie Gohmert (R–TX), and later as spokesman for House Republican Whip Roy Blunt (R-MO).

Snead regularly appears as a political commentator on Fox News and MSNBC. He is a cofounder of FamousDC.com, which has grown into a digital media empire. A member of the National Press Foundation board, he chairs the annual awards dinner that helps raise funds to train journalists. In addition to all of this, Snead is known in Washington for his unique ability to draw connections among professionals throughout the city.

A native of Centre, Alabama, Amos lives on Capitol Hill with this wife and three children.

JAIME HARRISON

A first-generation graduate with a BA from Yale University and a Juris Doctor from Georgetown University Law Center, Jaime is currently the associate chair and counselor of the Democratic National Committee. He previously served as the chair of the South Carolina Democratic Party, the first African American to hold the position.

Hailing from Orangeburg, South Carolina, Jaime was raised by his grandparents and young mom. While in college he interned with Senator Fritz Hollings and served as a Congressional Black Caucus Foundation intern for Congressman James Clyburn. Jaime also participated in the Congressional Black Caucus Institute Political Boot Camp.

He was the first African American to serve as executive director of the US House Democratic Caucus. In 2007, Jaime went on to serve as counsel and director of floor operations for House Majority Whip James Clyburn. Following his time on Capitol Hill, Jaime moved to the private sector at the Podesta Group, overseeing the firm's transportation practice.

Among many honors, he has been recognized as one of Roll Call's Fabulous 50 staffers on Capitol Hill, The Hill's "35 Stellar Staffers Under 35," one of the National Bar Association and IMPACT's "Top 40 lawyers under 40," and honored in the Root 100 black influencers under 45. Before entering politics, Jaime worked in education serving as chief operations officer and director of program development for the College Summit, a national nonprofit organization that assists low-income students enroll in college. Jaime also taught ninth grade social studies at his high school alma mater, Orangeburg-Wilkinson High.

Harrison has regularly appeared as a commentator on CNN and MSNBC. He lives in Columbia, South Carolina, with his wife and son.

INDEX

All rights reserved.
Published in the United States by Ten Speed Press,
an imprint of the Crown Publishing Group, a division
of Penguin Random House LLC, New York.
www.crownpublishing.com
www.tenspeed.com

Ten Speed Press and the Ten Speed Press colophon are registered trademarks
of Penguin Random House LLC.

Library of Congress Cataloging-in-Publication Data

Names: Harrison, Jaime R., author. | Snead, Amos, author.

Title: Climbing the Hill : how to build a career in politics and make a difference /
by Jaime R. Harrison and Amos Snead.

Description: First edition. | New York : Ten Speed Press, 2018. | Includes index.

Identifiers: LCCN 2018002474| ISBN 9780399581939 (paperback) |
ISBN 9780399581946 (ebk)

Subjects: LCSH: Political science—Vocational guidance—United States. |
Vocational guidance—United States. | Career development—United States. |

BISAC: BUSINESS & ECONOMICS / Careers / Job Hunting. | POLITICAL SCIENCE /

Government / Local. | POLITICAL SCIENCE / Political Process / Elections.

Classification: LCC JA88.U6 H37 2018 | DDC 324.2/20973—dc23

LC record available at https://lccn.loc.gov/2018002474

Trade Paperback ISBN: 978-0-399-58193-9
eBook ISBN: 978-0-399-58194-6

Design by Michelle Li

Printed in the United States

10 9 8 7 6 5 4 3 2 1

First Edition